Gardens Without Soil

House Plants, Vegetables, and Flowers

Gardens Without Soil

House Plants, Vegetables, and Flowers

JACK KRAMER

DRAWINGS BY
Charles Hoeppner
Robert A. Johnson

CHARLES SCRIBNER'S SONS   *New York*

Acknowledgments

I wish to express thanks to Robert Huston of the Department of Soils and Plant Nutrition of the University of California, who volunteered information on hydroponics and showed me and my photographer through their research areas.

I would also like to thank Richard Tracy of the Sacramento Bee Newspaper for his help about hydroponics, and several commercial growers throughout California; to them, too, a special thanks for their information about the plants they were growing and answers to my questions.

Jack Kramer

Library of Congress Cataloging in Publication Data

Kramer, Jack, 1927-
    Gardens without soil.

    1. Hydroponics. I. Title.
SB126.5.K7   631.5′85   75-22408
ISBN 0-684-14425-5

1 3 5 7 9 11 13 15 17 19 MD/C 20 18 16 14 12 10 8 6 4 2

Printed in the United States of America

Contents

Gardening Without Soil

When you start growing plants without soil in water solutions, you will think your brown thumb has turned green. And it will. Even the beginning gardener, as well as the experienced one, can grow house plants, vegetables, and flowers in water solutions. There is no messy soil to bother with, no repotting, and no worry about whether you are giving plants too much or not enough food and water. And for those folks with imagination there is a dividend: in handsome containers, soil-less house plants can be stellar decoration in home or apartment.

Once the initial setup is done—type of plant and kind of container—you supply the nutrient solutions to maintain healthy plants. But soil-less gardening in itself is no miracle worker—you will still have to provide good cultural practices to keep plants growing and in this book we show and tell you how to do it. While many plants will respond to this type of gardening, we concentrate on popular house plants, vegetables and some flowers.

Soil-less culture, practiced as early as the 1700's, and sometimes called hydroculture, is hardly new and is now enjoying a deserved renaissance because it is a relatively simple way of having plants without mess or fuss. Here, then, is a beginner's guide to this unique type of gardening (still another facet of the amazing plant world), so you can have plants of all kinds all year long.

Jack Kramer

ONE

Soil-less Gardening

Growing plants in water solutions is not new; as long ago as 1700 this type of gardening was practiced in England. Through the years solution gardening, or soil-less gardening (hydroponics), as it is technically called, has been used mainly by commercial vegetable and cut flower growers. The word hydroponics is derived from the Greek *hudor*, meaning water, and *ponos*, meaning work. In this book we shall use the term soil-less gardening to denote the hydroponic method of gardening.

Only recently has the average gardener recognized the advantages of soil-less gardening. You yourself have probably prac-

While many types of house plants will grow well in water and gravel it is far better to have plants in nutrient solutions so there is always food available to the plant. Here, Philodendron does well in plain water and gravel. (Photo by the author)

For commercial growing aqua culture is often used for tomato growing and with excellent results as shown in this photo. In this case, gravel is not necessary to hold plants upright but rather flat wooden tops with holes are used to keep plants vertical. Nutrient solutions are pumped in from tubes at left. (Photo by Clark Photo Graphics)

ticed home gardening minus soil without realizing it. Have you ever grown a house plant like a Philodendron in just water and gravel in a glass jar? This is a form of soil-less gardening. In aqua gardens, plants are set into containers that hold aggregates —gravel, sand—rather than soil, and water and nutrients are applied to the aggregates on a regular basis. Or plants are merely suspended in grids or holders (to keep them upright) in tanks or metal drums of nutrient solution. The aggregate method is better for home gardening because it entails less work and preparation and looks better aesthetically.

The rate of application of nutrients depends upon climate and the plants being grown (this is discussed in later chapters). You can make your own nutrient solutions from chemicals, or buy prepackaged solutions from suppliers. (See list at end of book.) In either case you mix a specific amount of nutrient salts with a specific amount of water to feed plants with necessary nutrients they need in order to grow.

ADVANTAGES

If you have grown plants in soil in pots, you already know that in a few to several months plants deplete soil of nutrients. Your plants start to starve to death, so you either apply plant foods to supply the necessary nutrients or repot plants in fresh soil. With soil-less gardening you do not have to fuss with messy soils or repot plants in fresh soil. And you do not have to haul soil into the home, which can be especially difficult if you live in an apartment. Cost is a factor too; today soil is expensive, but gravel— the medium used to hold plants upright in containers—is still

In nutrient solutions plants get a constant supply of foods to grow. Here you can see healthy roots and lush growth of spinach plants. (Photo by Clark Photo Graphics)

cheap. And with plants in soil you never know just what hidden insects are buried in the pot; with soil-less gardening this worry is eliminated.

Growing plants in water solutions is an inexpensive way to have all kinds of plants year-round, whether vegetables, flowers, or house plants. And as a hobby it promises a great deal of satisfaction for a small amount of expense and effort. Healthy, aqua-grown plants year-round are bound to be more lively than plants that may die because their soil has been depleted of nutrients.

Other Considerations

Although growing plants in a water solution is less work and

Seeds embedded between blotters and doused with water result in sprouting —another form of hydroponic gardening. (Photo by USDA)

worry than growing them in soil, it should not be considered a shortcut to successful gardening. Nutrient solutions alone will not make plants flourish or your home become a verdant greenery. You yourself must assume some responsibility: you must administer solutions, put plants in proper light, see that temperatures are optimum, and protect plants from disease and insects. When you grow plants in water solution you eliminate much guesswork as to how much and when to water them and how much food to give and when, but you still *must* provide other cultural necessities to get plants growing bigger and better. Cultural requirements for water-grown plants are somewhat different than for plants in soil; the ways and means of soil-less gardening are explained in future chapters.

You do not have to have any knowledge of chemistry to do soil-less gardening. Some basic mathematics is necessary, but all you really need is just a little adventure in your soul and some curiosity. For example, recently some commercial manufacturers have been selling a Magic Plant Starter; it looks like a blotter with seeds adhered to it. Just add water; it really works. In fact, if you embedded seeds between two blotters, saturated the blotters with water, and put them in a dish with a Baggie over them (to assure humidity) you would have had your first taste of a form of hydroponic gardening.

WHAT TO GROW

Just what kind of plants you grow depends on your available space and your personal tastes. You can start most of the midget vegetables successfully in a window space. Then move tubs and boxes (not too large) onto a back porch or balcony during the summer. If your growing area is very limited, use just a few foliage plants in decorative containers for an attractive aqua garden. Put the plants in gravel, supply them with nutrients solution on a regular basis, and you will have a unique garden. Even

Redwood boxes are excellent for soil-less gardens and flowers and vegetables can be grown. The boxes are outdoors on a patio deck in warm weather and taken indoors in inclement weather. (Photo by author)

This handsome outdoor cactus and succulent garden is planted in gravel. A nutrient solution is supplied to give plants necessary food. (Photo by author)

A Popular Planter

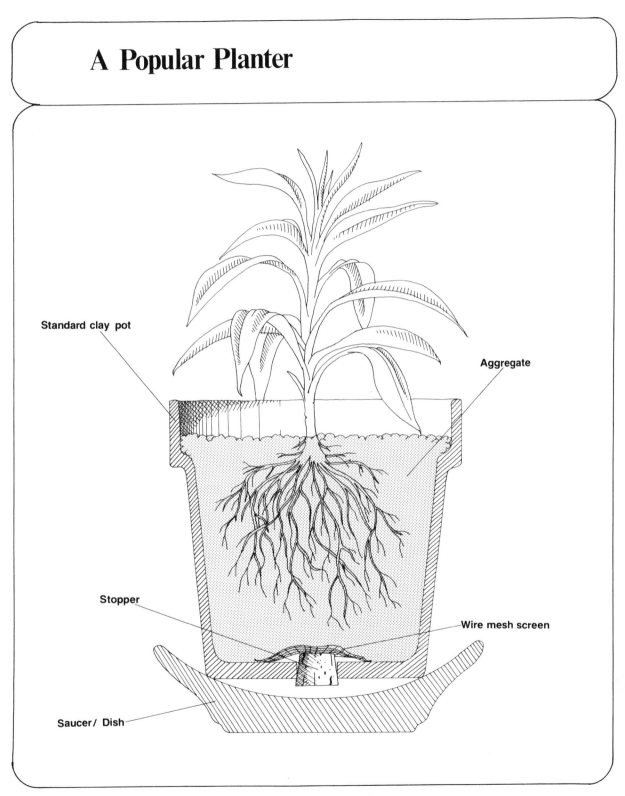

Standard clay pot

Aggregate

Stopper

Wire mesh screen

Saucer/ Dish

Bob Johnson

For a very decorative look, house plants can be grown in ornamental containers. Here we see Dizygotheca, Dracaenas, and a Bromeliad at right. In place of ordinary white gravel, oval black stones are used to provide a more finished look. (Photo courtesy Architectural Pottery Co.)

just one fine Philodendron or ti-plant in a handsome glass container can be grown if that is all you want or have room for.

I generally use soil-less gardening for house plants in decorative containers, dwarf annuals, and perennials, and some of the midget vegetables: a basket of lettuce at the kitchen sink, some radishes and cucumbers on a trellis at a window. (*Standard*-sized vegetables and annuals and perennials should be grown in a greenhouse.) For the average hobbyist this is the best way to start and get your feet wet; later you can expand your plans and plants into more elaborate soil-less gardening setups, such as greenhouses.

TWO

How Soil-less Gardening Works

You could just buy one of the commercial Magic Plant Starters, or just plunk a cutting of a plant in water in a jar to have some green plants for the home. But soil-less gardening is better because it provides a continuous feeding program, so you should know just how and why hydroponics work. This chapter presents basic information about plant growth, nutrient assimilation, and what and where you can grow plants. None of this data is technical and in the long run it will help you understand better the workings of *all* plants, whether they are grown in water solution or in soil.

PLANTS AND NUTRIENTS

A plant is an entity within itself, capable of changing raw food material into living tissue. Plants cannot ingest solid or organic food materials; they get their nourishment from gases (oxygen and carbon dioxide) in the air and from solutions of organic (mineral) salts or chemicals in water. The mineral salts in combination with water are absorbed by plant root hairs by a process known as osmosis; the plants make living tissue from these nutrients of salts and water by using light. In aqua solutions plants receive optimum nutrition because the roots are always in contact with moisture, unlike a potted plant in caked soil, so the air necessary to carry water to roots is already established.

Because plants grow toward light, they must stand firmly vertical. Soil supplies this support, but with soil-less gardening *you* must supply the proper devices to keep plants vertical: a good base of gravel, cinders, or any inert substance so roots and stems can breathe.

Seeds have been started in a glass container with gravel and vermiculite. They are slightly embedded in the medium and with minimum care will germinate to furnish new plants. (Photo by Jack Barnick)

NUTRIENTS AND GROWTH

Within soil gardening, it is difficult to determine just how much nutrients are in the soil at any given time. Besides oxygen and carbon dioxide from the air, eleven different elements are necessary for good plant growth: nitrogen, phosphorus, potassium, calcium, manganese, sulfur, iron, magnesium, boron, zinc, and copper. In soil-less gardening you yourself administer these necessary elements in a balanced formula, so you can control them easily (formulas are discussed in Chapter 3). There is no waste or leaching out of plant food; there is no guesswork or worry about watering. What is important is following some simple rules about nutrient solutions and how to apply them. (You can buy packaged hydroponic elements from suppliers and just add water instead of mixing your own solutions.)

Plants in water solutions grow all, not just part of, the time, so

Essentials for Growth

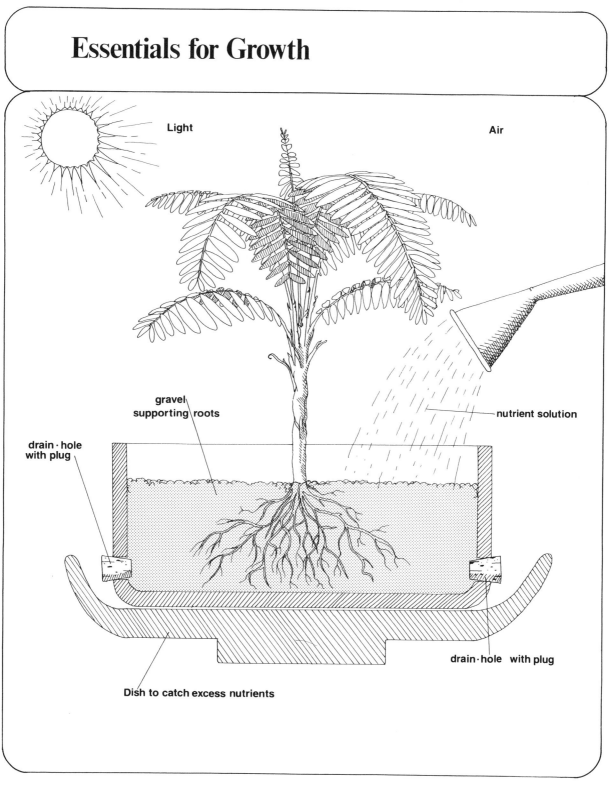

Light

Air

gravel
supporting roots

nutrient solution

drain·hole
with plug

drain·hole with plug

Dish to catch excess nutrients

Bob Johnson

they must have a plentiful supply of water; good light to assimilate the nutrients; and humidity, air, and a buoyant atmosphere. In other words, you are striving for a balanced program of all elements to produce healthy plants. You can get good results from growing certain house plants in just water, that is, without solutions, but eventually the water becomes stagnant, and usually without adequate nutrients plants wither and eventually die, sometimes in a few weeks. However, plants in water solutions keep on growing to become mature specimens because they are receiving all necessary nutrients.

WHAT AND WHERE YOU CAN GROW

There is really very little limitation as to what kinds of plants you can grow by the soil-less gardening method. As mentioned in Chapter 1, most house plants do very well; indeed, some, like Philodendrons and Cacti, grow better in gravel than in soil. Midget vegetables also grow fast (a prerequisite for good farming), thus producing bountiful crops for your eating pleasure. For example, cucumbers and tomatoes can be grown successfully by even the novice gardener.

Starting plants from seeds, which is becoming a popular gardening method because of the high prices of plants, is easier with hydroponics than starting the plants in soil. Starting the seeds of annuals and perennials can produce many lovely bouquets of blooms for the home. If you have some prize plants and want new plants from them you can start cuttings, too. (See Chapter 7.)

Actually, just what you grow depends only on the space you have; like house plant gardens, your solution gardens can occupy any area where there is some natural light. If you have a small greenhouse, there is no end to the plants you can grow. (See Chapter 8.) A 5- x 10-foot outdoor area (backyard, porch) provides enough room for dozens of plants.

Cacti are not often thought of for soil-less gardening but they do very well in gravel and indeed seem to grow better than in soil. Crown rot which strikes some cacti is not as liable to start in a gravel base. (Photo by author)

If decorative gardening is more your thing, aqua gardens can be arranged on a windowsill, in hanging containers above windows, in dish gardens, in trays or pots on tables or carts. Soil-less gardening can be done in a house or an apartment or the greenhouse—almost any place where there is sufficient space.

THE HUNT FOR CONTAINERS

Finding suitable containers for soil-less gardening can be fun.

Preparing a Hydroponic Planter

1. Select or build a water-tight container with drain-holes and stoppers.

treated wood or galvanized metal

drain·hole   stoppers

2. Fill with aggregate (stoppers in place).

3. Water thoroughly and evenly, then drain to settle gravel.

4. Plant seedlings, and add solution with rose can.

stoppers in place

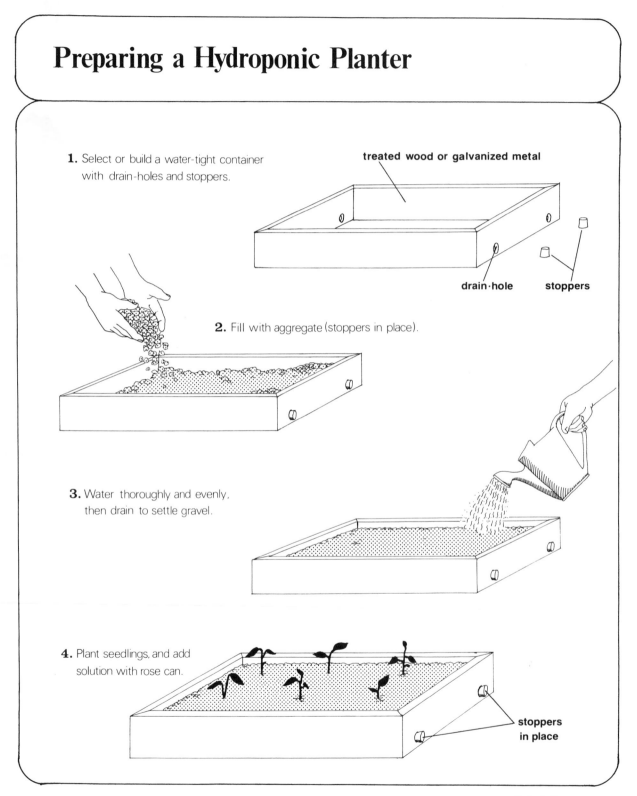

Bob Johnson

This hydroponic home unit is offered by Miracle Gardens of New York City. It comes with containers, nutrients, and pump. (Photo courtesy Miracle Gardens Inc.)

Use your imagination; there are many kinds of kitchen apparatus —for example, teapots and crocks—that will make fine decorative gardens. You can also grow plants in commercial plastic trays available from suppliers, or make your own plant containers from wood or concrete. There are many, many kinds of vessels, some decorative, some more utilitarian; what you use depends on what you are growing.

Tanks or vats with complicated recirculating systems for nutrient solutions are not necessary. However, you can set up a container

A croton grows in gravel culture and needs watering with a nutrient solution only every third day. This heavy glass container is ideal for plants because holes can be drilled in the bottom for drainage. (Photo by author)

Vegetables can be grown in simple containers. This is a plastic tray with gravel and nutrient solutions are applied every day. Lush growth and firm stems are the result. (Photo by author)

within a container for a hydroponic unit and use a small recirculating pump to administer air and nutrient solution to the aggregate. (See photo.)

THREE

What You Need

The basic needs for soil-less gardening are simple: a container, a bin or tray under it, aggregate, light, suitable temperatures, air, and the nutrient solution. The container may be a dish or pot, tub, trough, or pan. The aggregate or supporting medium may be gravel, sand, vermiculite, cinders, pumice, or even broken pots. You will also need a watering can, glass bottles for nutrient solutions, a small hand spade, a kitchen scale for measuring chemicals, plugs or corks for drainage holes, string to stake vertical plants, and stakes to act as trellises.

A container for a soil-less garden can be a household item too; here a fruit bowl is used. Note the small holes in the bowl. (Photo by author)

CONTAINERS

I believe that one reason soil-less gardening has not been done more in recent years is the problem of just what to grow the plants in. But there are many suitable containers: window boxes, regular flower pots with plugs in drainage holes, wooden or plastic metal planters. In this chapter we include some drawings of special boxes and housings you can make quickly at home.

Usually, the type of plant (quantity too) will dictate just what kind of container to use. A decorative pot or standard clay one is fine for house plants. So is a kitchen container such as the fruit bowl with holes shown in the photograph. For vegetables, use tubs or barrels or large plastic bins.

A bromeliad grows in aqua culture in a clay pot. Bromeliads, like cacti, are subject to crown rot and do better in gravel than in a soil base. The drain hole in the pot is plugged with a cork and removed every third day to leach out excess nutrient solutions. (Photo by author)

Containers From Salvage Stores

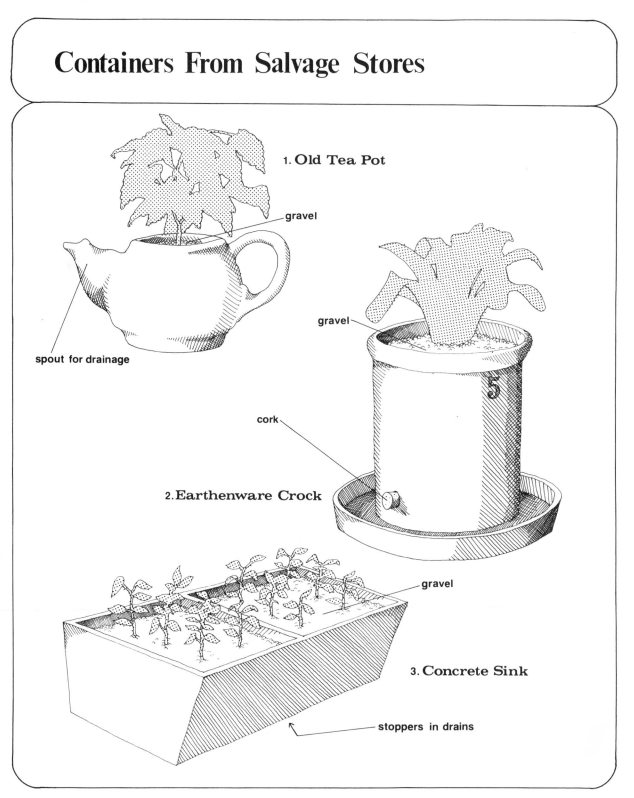

1. Old Tea Pot

gravel

spout for drainage

gravel

cork

2. Earthenware Crock

gravel

3. Concrete Sink

stoppers in drains

Bob Johnson

Any container should be at least 8 inches deep, less than 30 inches wide, and have drainage holes. (Glass stores in your area will drill holes in ceramic and glass containers.) You must fit the drainage holes with small plugs or stoppers so you can change the water solutions (the right solutions are necessary for adequate root development). Hardware stores generally carry a supply of stoppers or corks. Or use floral clay at florist shops to plug drain holes. However, even with stoppers in holes, there will be some seepage, so you must have a tray or pan under the con-

A nasturtium starting life in a soil-less garden. These plants thrive on heavy feeding and are relatively easy to grow this way. (Photo by author)

Containers You Can Buy

1. **Tea or Coffee Urn**

gravel

spigot for drainage

gravel

stopper

2. **Ceramic Pot**

gravel

3. **Glass Dish**

cork
in small drilled hole

Bob Johnson

Corks of various diameters are obtainable at hardware stores and are used to stop up drain holes. They are removed every second or third day to let excess spent nutrient solution drain away. (Photo by author)

If you cannot find stoppers or corks at hardware stores you can use florist clay. Simply mold the clay into the drain holes and remove clay when necessary. (Photo by author)

tainer. Some ornamental glass containers simply cannot be drilled, so omit the holes; uproot the plant from the aggregate once a month to furnish it with adequate nutrients. (This is the least suitable way of growing plants in water solutions.)

Window Boxes

Window boxes are ideal for plants. The commercially made ones—plastic, metal, or wood—work as well for solution gardening as they do for soil gardening. In place of the soil simply substitute gravel, and find suitable stoppers for the drainage holes. That is about all there is to it. Or make a window box yourself. Cut five pieces of redwood to size, and then join them with screws at the corners. Insert polyethylene plastic in the box to hold the contents, or have galvanized trays with drainage holes made to fit into the boxes.

Terra Cotta Pots

Terra cotta pots make fine housings for a single plant. Find a suitable stopper, and fill the pot with gravel. There are dozens of styles of clay pots on the market, but select the shallow pots, say, 6 to 8 inches deep rather than very deep ones because in pots, great accumulations of aggregates can become compacted and hinder the aeration which is essential to the good growth of plants. Use large-diameter pots (to 20 inches) for several plants; an 8- to 10-inch diameter pot is fine for a few plants.

Concrete Containers

Homemade concrete containers are fine housings for solution gardens. Get wood framing for the size of the box desired; the concrete mix can be Sakrete commercial mix, which requires only water. Pour the mix into the wooden forms, put a presoaked standard terra cotta pot into the mix, and fill the pot with more concrete to the top of the frame. When the concrete is firm, scrub

Containers You Can Make

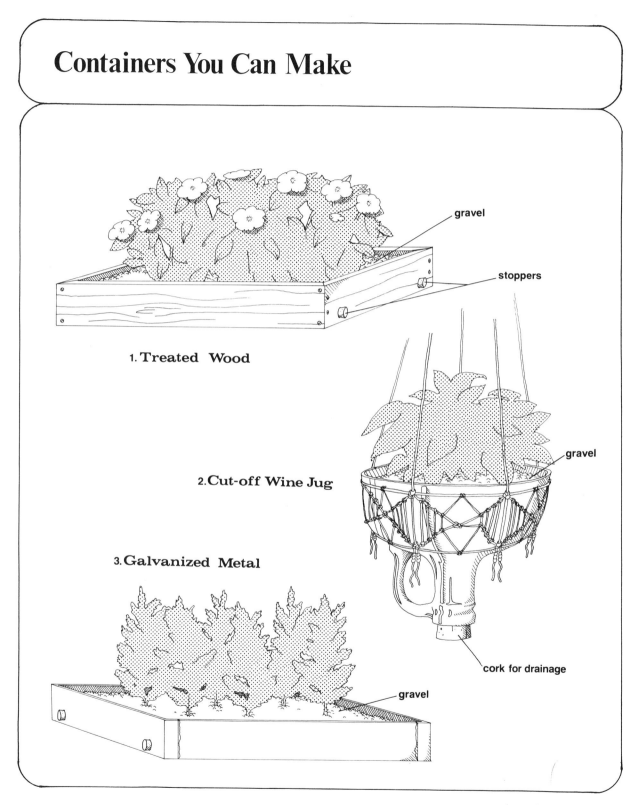

gravel

stoppers

1. Treated Wood

2. Cut-off Wine Jug

gravel

3. Galvanized Metal

cork for drainage

gravel

Bob Johnson

it with a wire brush. After 24 hours, strip away the wooden forms and remove the pot. Run water over the surface, and scrub the surface with a wire brush.

Another type of concrete container can be made by using two cardboard boxes. One should be small enough to fit inside the larger one, with 2 inches of space between the cartons. First pour 2 inches of concrete mix into the bottom of the larger carton. Tamp down, and insert the smaller carton. Now pour and tamp the mix between the two cartons to make the walls of the planter. After 24 hours, remove the cardboard forms, and let the concrete dry slowly for about 2 days. Then use a chisel to shape the container. Scrub the container with a wire brush, and wet it down several times before using.

AGGREGATES

Once you have made, purchased, or found a container, you must fill it with a bed of aggregate, to 2 inches from the top. Use sand, gravel, small pebbles, or broken pot pieces as the aggregate—any inert material is suitable. Avoid materials like peat, sphagnum, or osmunda for growing plants because they have unbalanced compositions and generally retain water much too long, making a compacted medium that can be harmful to plants. Sawdust is free, but it can compact in time.

Sand

Sand has long been used for soil-less gardening. The best type is fairly coarse so water and air can circulate between the grains. Fine sand is liable to become compacted and thwart good drainage. Sand size is rated by mesh. Sands under a 30 mesh should not be used without the addition of coarser materials (gravel). Buy sand at local building yards or from garden centers.

Making a Concrete Planter

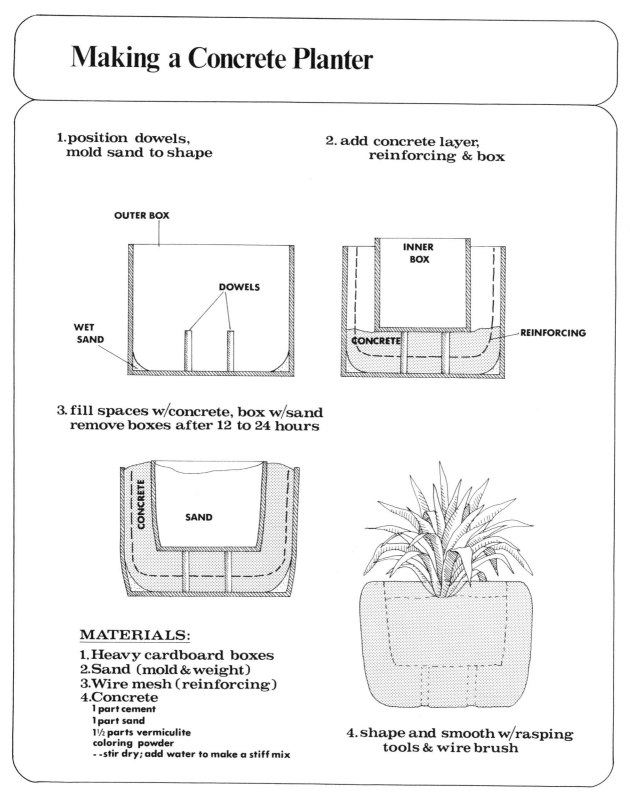

1. position dowels,
   mold sand to shape

2. add concrete layer,
   reinforcing & box

OUTER BOX

DOWELS

WET
SAND

INNER
BOX

CONCRETE

REINFORCING

3. fill spaces w/concrete, box w/sand
   remove boxes after 12 to 24 hours

CONCRETE

SAND

MATERIALS:
1. Heavy cardboard boxes
2. Sand (mold & weight)
3. Wire mesh (reinforcing)
4. Concrete
   1 part cement
   1 part sand
   1½ parts vermiculite
   coloring powder
   - -stir dry; add water to make a stiff mix

4. shape and smooth w/rasping
   tools & wire brush

Bob Johnson

Gravel

Gravel, small broken stones or crushed rocks of various types, is the most popular aggregate. The particles range from $\frac{1}{16}$ to $\frac{1}{2}$ inch in diameter and come in various colors, mostly gray, although white crushed stone looks quite attractive. You can also

Gravel such as this is excellent as an aggregate for soil-less gardening. Before using gravel wash in clear water. The material is inexpensive and a good medium. (Photo by author)

A close-up shot of gravel showing the many faceted sides of the stones and demonstrating the air spaces between the stones. This provides aeration in the medium which is essential to carry nutrients to plant roots. (Photo by author)

use aquarium gravel, but it is somewhat expensive. Wash gravel first before filling the container.

Vermiculite

Vermiculite is a sterile, lightweight, highly absorbent material that retains water and air. Some growers use only vermiculite, but I find it is better to mix it with some gravel. Vermiculite's high water-retaining property may keep plants too damp in winter, causing fungus and bacterial growth. Buy standard-grade vermiculite at suppliers.

Cinders

There are many kinds of cinders for growing plants in water solutions. Soak soft and hard coal cinders overnight, and then wash them before placing them in containers. Fine cinders can compact in water, so use heavier, larger pieces to enable air and water to reach plants' roots. Cinders are free, of course.

WATER

The water that comes from your tap is quite suitable for solution gardening; no special water is needed. Any water suitable for drinking is fine for growing plants. Occasionally someone reports that excessively salty water may be injurious to plants, but this premise is not valid. As long as there are good drainage and free movement, even salty water is suitable for your plants. Hard water, that is, water which contains a great deal of calcium salts and magnesium, is fine too, but water containing too much chlorine can be injurious to plants. However, most water in this country does not contain excessive chlorine.

If you are leery about your water supply, place some cut flowers in a glass of water for a few days. If you can see no ill effects, the water may be presumed fine for plants. Or obtain an analysis of the water supply: call your city water company or, in rural areas, the agricultural department.

AVAILABILITY OF NUTRIENT SALTS

Some of the chemicals for mixing formulas, such as ammonium sulfate and superphosphate, are sold at garden centers and nurseries. They come in tidy bags and if kept dry can be used over a long period of time. Other chemicals, potassium nitrate for example, are not as easy to find. First check a pharmacy to see if they have materials; if not, consult the yellow pages of the phone book under the "chemical supplier" listing. These companies generally have everything you need but unfortunately usually only sell in large quantities, hardly feasible for the home gardener. Still, they may sell you the amount you need or be able to direct you to a local source that does have the chemicals in smaller amounts.

Prepackaged nutrients salts made specifically for hydroponic gardening are sold by various suppliers. In the near future I am sure more companies will offer hydroponic solutions for home use, as well as the proper containers and water devices.

FOUR

Nutrient Solutions and How to Use Them

Plants need a balanced diet of nutrients to prosper; in soil they utilize the nutrients from the soil. But in soil-less gardening *you* must supply the balanced diet to sustain plant growth. The kind of feeding formula or mixture you use depends on the kinds of plants being grown, the size of the container, and related factors like light, humidity, and air circulation. There are dozens of different hydroponic feeding formulas; just which one you use and how you apply it will determine your success with soil-less gardening.

WHAT NUTRIENT SOLUTIONS ARE

The nutrients you will be working with (unless you buy pre-packaged hydroponic food) are nitrogen, potassium, phosphorus, calcium, sulfur, and magnesium. The trace elements are iron, copper, zinc, manganese, and boron. Each element plays a part in the development of a plant, so it is wise to know what each one does:

Nitrogen is the building block of plants; it produces good foliage and firm stems and leaves, thus making plants robust and strong.

Phosphorus stimulates root development and growth and helps hasten the ripening process.

Potassium is vital for photosynthesis, an absolute function of any plant if it is to live. (Photosynthesis is the process by which plants utilize light to form carbohydrates.)

42

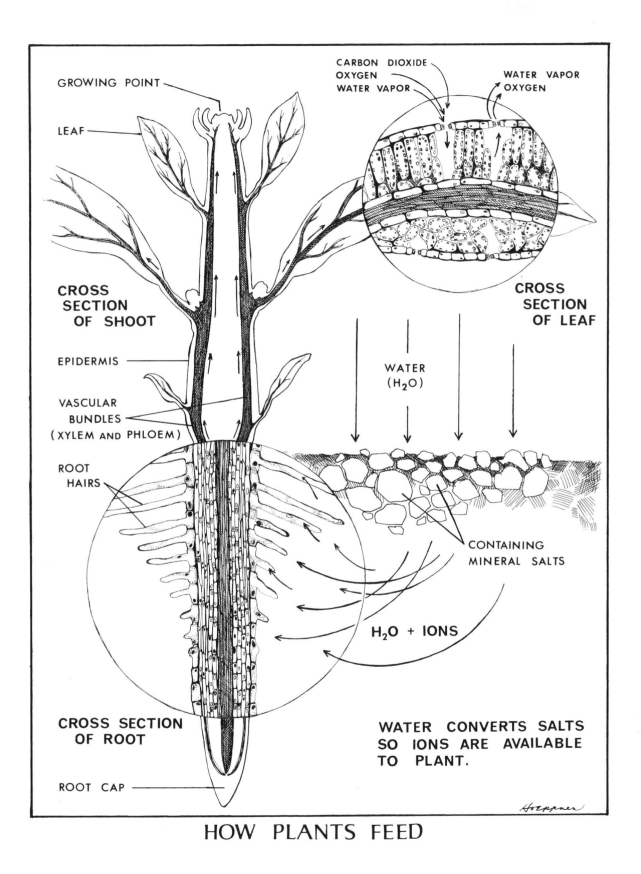

HOW PLANTS FEED

Nutrient solution is piped into these vat containers and plants are held in place in holes in the boards. In such a setup plants are assured of all proper elements to stimulate growth. (Photo by Clark Photo Graphics)

Calcium promotes early root formation, influences the intake of other plant foods, and encourages good bacterial action.

Sulfur is used in the development of such essential organic compounds as proteins and affects the chlorophyll production of a plant.

Magnesium works in conjunction with phosphorus and stimulates the assimilation of phosphorus by the plant. It is essential in the formation of chlorophyll.

Iron also helps in chlorophyll production; without iron, no chlorophyll is formed.

Copper and *zinc* regulate the oxidation and reduction processes. Copper also helps develop flavor in fruits and vegetables; zinc is necessary for the formation of chlorophyll.

Healthy plants that get sufficient nutrients produce healthy roots as seen in this photo. (Photo by Clark Photo Graphics)

Manganese is necessary in the photosynthesis process.

Boron helps young tissues become strong and speeds up the absorption of potassium.

FORMULAS

Although many different formulas have been developed through

Some hydroponic chemicals such as aluminum sulfate and ammonium phosphate are at nurseries; others at pharmacies or chemical companies. (Photo by author)

the years by hydroponic researchers, they all have the same objective: to supply plants with the vital foods they need to grow. Generally the actual choice of fertilizer salts is not as important as the balanced concentration of the necessary elements. In commercial growing, precise and stringent rules regarding solutions and their application are a must to produce the most in the least amount of time—a heavy good crop. However, in home culture a few mistakes will not cause undue harm. Your plants will soon let you know if your chemical formulas are awry; the symptoms of over- or underfeeding (unbalanced proportions of nutrients salts) are discussed later. Just as soil mixes vary in nutrient content, so will water solution formulas. You will have to experiment to achieve the final formulas that work for your plants in your home conditions.

Whether you buy your nutrient mixes ready-made or blend your own at home depends on your own personal choice. Being naturally curious, I prefer to weigh out my own nutrient salts on a kitchen scale, mix them together and store them, and use them as I need them for the plants. It is also cheaper than buying commercial hydroponic foods.

For general use the following mixtures will provide excellent results for most plants:

PACKAGED CHEMICALS OR SALTS	NUTRIENTS SUPPLIED	AMOUNT OF EACH (OUNCES)
Sodium nitrate	Nitrogen	10
Potassium sulfate	Potassium, sulfur	3½
Superphosphate	Phosphorus, calcium	5
Magnesium sulfate (Epsom salts)	Magnesium, sulfur	3
Iron sulfate	Iron	¼

Use approximately five teaspoons of formula to five gallons of water.

Another mixture, recommended by the United States Department of Agriculture, is shown at the top of page 48.

PACKAGED CHEMICALS OR SALTS	NUTRIENTS SUPPLIED	AMOUNT OF EACH (OUNCES)
*Ammonium sulfate	Nitrogen, sulfur	1½
Potassium nitrate	Nitrogen, potassium	9
Monocalcium phosphate	Phosphorus, calcium	4
Magnesium sulfate (Epsom salts)	Magnesium, sulfur	6
Calcium sulfate	Calcium, sulfur	7
Iron sulfate	Iron	pinch

*Or sodium nitrate

Use approximately five teaspoons of formula to five gallons of water.

In the above mixtures, the trace or minor elements such as manganese, boron, zinc, copper, and minute amounts of other elements will probably be supplied by the impurities in the water supply. However, the commercial or packaged chemicals will already contain these minor elements. Thus it is unnecessary to add them to the solution. However, if you use pure-grade chemicals in making solutions, you will have to add some manganese sulfate, copper sulfate, boric acid crystals, and iron chelate (1 teaspoon). Add ⅓ fluid ounce to 10 gallons of water. Boric acid crystals dissolve in boiling water; manganese and copper dissolve in hot water.

Here is a breakdown of the main packaged chemicals or salts and what they supply to plants:

Sodium nitrate is the usual source of nitrogen in nutrient solutions and has approximately 15% nitrogen. The sodium is not required by plants but appears to have no bad effects on plants.

Potassium nitrate supplies both potassium and nitrogen but may be expensive. It contains about 13% nitrogen and 44% potash.

Potassium sulfate gives potassium to plants and contains about 50%.

Superphosphate is the principal source of phosphorus; it contains 16 to 18% phosphorus.

Magnesium sulfate (Epsom salts) is the cheapest form of magnesium (16%).

Trace elements, when not supplied as impurities in the water or chemicals, are usually added as sulfates:
    Copper sulfate
    Manganese sulfate
    Zinc sulfate
    Boron (derived from boric acid crystals)

PREPARING SOLUTIONS

To prepare the solution, weigh out amounts on a kitchen scale, and then put them one by one into a bowl or whatever. Mix them together well, using a wooden spoon or a pestle—the idea is to break down any lumps. The mixture is completed when you have a fine powder. Now store in a dry container with a cover; never allow nutrients to get damp or wet before storing. Also, all individual fertilizers, tools, and containers should be absolutely dry. If you want to make a larger amount of nutrients, simply multiply all ingredients by 2, 3, and so on. Add small amounts of the formula to water, generally 5 teaspoonfuls of formula to 5 gallons of water for the completed nutrient solution. [If you would rather not prepare your own solutions, buy the commercially packaged hydroponic mixtures from chemical houses, nurseries, and so on (see list of suppliers at end of book). Follow the directions on the package to the letter. Do not try to substitute packaged fertilizers such as 10-10-5 for solutions because they do not contain all necessary ingredients for good hydroponic growing.]

APPLYING SOLUTIONS

Once the container is set up and plants are in place, apply the first application of nutrient fertilizer to the surface of the aggregate. To avoid disturbing the aggregate, use the old-fashioned type of watering can, one with a metal spout that has many small holes in the spout. Sprinkle evenly and thoroughly so the solution will penetrate all parts of the aggregate. (The aggregate should be like a moist sponge.) The rate of application of the solution de-

In this photo, small plants are shown started in vats with nutrient solution and they do very well. Almost any kind of container that has facilities for piping solution in and out is fine. (Photo by Clark Photo Graphics)

Various Methods of Applying Nutrient Solution

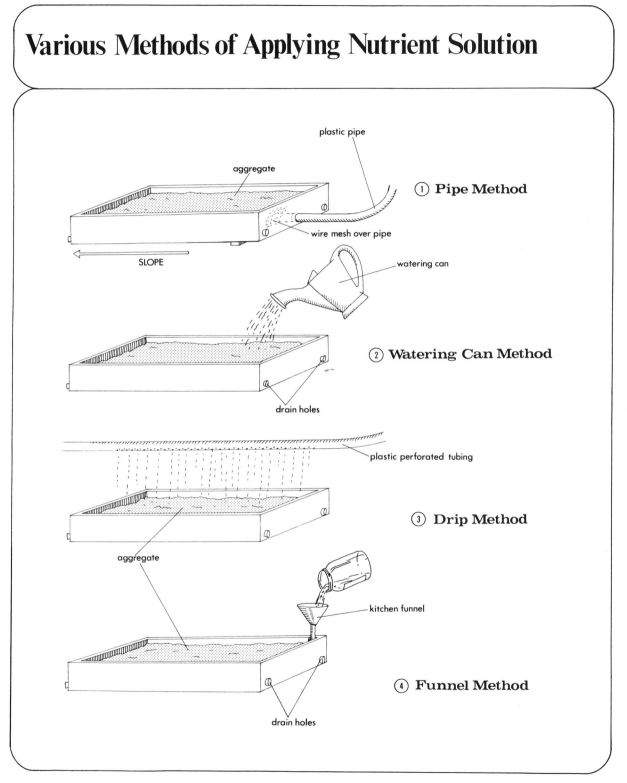

plastic pipe

aggregate

① **Pipe Method**

wire mesh over pipe

SLOPE

watering can

② **Watering Can Method**

drain holes

plastic perforated tubing

③ **Drip Method**

aggregate

kitchen funnel

aggregate

④ **Funnel Method**

drain holes

Bob Johnson

pends on climatic conditions and the plants being grown. Vegetables and flowers will require more frequent applications than, say, house plants. In very hot, dry areas, more solution is necessary than in damp, cool places. Generally, for most plants use two or three applications a week. In spring and summer, plants may need new solution every other day. In the fall, once or twice a week is sufficient, and in the winter, once a week is enough.

Make sure the growing medium never dries out. On the other hand, be careful that the medium never becomes waterlogged; that is, there should be no excess water standing above the aggregate surface line. Every third day or so (depending on the size of container), remove the drainage plugs and allow all unused water solution inside the bottom of the container to seep out into the saucer or tray. Discard the unused water to remove spent nutrients and toxic salts and to move air through the aggregate from the open holes to the surface of the medium, which benefits roots.

If you are using too much water and solution, your plants will soon tell you: they will start wilting because they are waterlogged. If this occurs, once every 2 weeks remove the plugs and leach the aggregate gently by pouring clear water onto the surface. Repeat several times to really remove all toxic salts. (See also the nutrient deficiency symptoms at the end of this chapter.)

pH

The pH indicates the amount of acid or alkalinity in the nutrient solution. Most plants prefer a neutral medium (pH 7); a pH below 7 indicates acidity, and a pH above 7 indicates alkalinity. In alkaline mediums, potash becomes less and less effective and eventually becomes locked in and of no use to the plant. In very acid mediums, the element aluminum becomes so active that it can become toxic to plants. Acidity controls three main functions: (1) it governs the availability of the food in the medium; (2) it determines which bacteria thrive in the medium; and (3) to some extent it affects the rate at which roots can take up moisture and leaves can manufacture food.

Raising or lowering the pH of soil can be a difficult process and generally must be done over a period of time. But in soil-less gardening it is far easier for you to adjust the pH to the optimum required for plants. To determine the pH of your growing medium—to be sure you are applying correct amounts of solution— use litmus paper (sold at suppliers). All you have to do is match the color of the test strip with an indicator chart.

Note: If the pH of the solution is maintained at approximately 5.5 to 6.0, a reasonable concentration of ammonia can be used without injury to plants. When the pH is increased, the rate of entry of ammonia into the plant is also increased, and the plant may become injured.

The best pH for most vegetable crops is between 6.6 and 6.8. If the pH is too low, add small amounts of phosphoric acid; if it is too high, add caustic potash. Add micronutrient solutions after new solutions have been pH-adjusted. This should adjust the pH of the growing medium in about 1 week.

NUTRIENT DEFICIENCY SYMPTOMS

Because plants live or die depending on the nutrient solution, you must know some general plant deficiency symptoms so you can make necessary adjustments in your formula:

1. If plants have light green foliage and growth seems stunted, or if leaves become almost yellow, you *must* add more nitrogen.

2. If there is delayed growth and the lower foliage turns yellow or very dark in color, the plants are not getting enough phosphorus.

3. If lower leaves are mottled near tips and margins and become brown, plants need more potassium.

Lush sugar beet is shown growing in drums at the University of California research department. These plants are in growth chambers with artificial light above them. (Photo by Clark Photo Graphics)

4. If leaves curl or pucker, plants are not getting enough magnesium.

5. If plants have poor bloom and spots appear on leaf surfaces, plants are not getting enough manganese.

Gravel allows good aeration, a vital part of successful soil-less gardening. Here a small cabbage grows well. (Photo by author)

6. If leaves are very light green and plants somewhat limp, they require more sulfur.

7. If leaves, especially young ones, are brown at tip or margins, plants need more calcium.

8. If stems are brittle or young leaves are stunted, plants need more boron.

AERATION

Aeration of the growing medium is vital if you want healthy plants. Oxygen must be present in the medium so a vigorous and healthy root system can grow. A poorly aerated medium retards root formation, and the plant becomes chlorotic through lack of iron because this element appears to be absorbed only by new roots. If the plant cannot absorb nutrients because of poor aeration, starvation symptoms occur: lack of color in leaves, to the point that they become dull and gray looking. Also, the plant wilts in bright light as transpiration becomes more rapid than absorption of water by the poorly developed roots.

Aeration also affects to some degree the amount of potassium absorbed by the plant. In a compacted medium carbon dioxide accumulates and harms plants.

FIVE

Care of Plants

Caring for plants in soil-less gardening is less complicated than caring for plants in soil, but some cultural rules and a knowledge of light, air circulation, humidity, and temperature are still necessary. Different kinds of plants require different care, but generally most plants will adapt to these conditions and grow if light is optimum. Air and humidity are prime considerations whether you grow plants in water solutions or in soil, and of course temperature is related to light. Cleanliness in growing areas and the prevention of insects are other aspects to consider when growing plants.

LIGHT

Without light, plants will not grow. Light is the deciding factor as to whether plants thrive or merely exist. For solution garden plants, average bright light, with a few hours of sunlight during the day if possible, is all that is necessary. It is important to remember that the more light plants have, the more quickly they will grow and assimilate foods. Thus, if light is very good at your aqua gardens, more frequent changing of solution will be necessary than if light is poor. During dull, cloudy days it is best not to add solutions; wait for days with bright light. Adding solutions on dull days does little for the plant because without adequate light it cannot assimilate the foods.

Generally, keep plants out of the intense summer sun, which will scorch and desiccate leaves. If plants are near windows, provide a screen or light curtain to prevent scorching; most window panes are wavy and can magnify sun rays, thus causing spots of intense sunlight that will scorch leaves.

57

A philodendron in a decorative soil-less garden; actually the fruit bowl shown earlier. (Photo by author)

For best results, place solution gardens near west or east exposures; avoid south windows because they can be very hot during the summer. Use north windows for plants that can, with little effort, tolerate low light levels and still live, such as Philodendrons, Aspidistras, and Peperomias.

TEMPERATURE AND AIR CIRCULATION

Most house plants are comfortable if you are and will adjust to average home temperatures of 55° to 75°F during the day, with a 10-degree drop at night. Very high temperatures along with poor light and dryness will kill plants quickly; too low temperatures coupled with too much moisture can cause mildew and bacterial diseases. And contrary to what many people think, lower nighttime temperatures benefit plants.

Most plants will not survive drafts from air conditioners or heat from radiators because either will cause havoc. Even drafts from doors can cause plants like Dieffenbachias to wilt overnight. But plants do need good air circulation because in nature, few plants grow in stagnant conditions. So try to keep a window open slightly in or near the growing area (even in winter). If this is impossible, use small fans at moderate speed to keep air circulating. The amount of fresh ventilated air will do wonders for plants, whereas a stagnant atmosphere will hinder them.

HUMIDITY

This is a general bugaboo for most plants—more plants die because of lack of humidity than because of any other factor. Humidity, the amount of moisture in the air, should be maintained at 30 to 50 percent for both you and your plants (and furniture). Plants grown with too high humidity are soft and succulent and contain a high percentage of water, thus wilting rapidly. Plants grown with too low humidity tend to be hard, with small leaves or leaves that drop. The plants simply cannot manufacture proteins; the growing regions gradually stop their activity, and the plants become woody. A hygrometer, an instrument that measures the moisture in the air, is an excellent, inexpensive investment (hygrometers are available at any hardware store).

With soil-less gardening some humidity is furnished by the evaporation of water on the gravel, but this might not be enough moisture, especially in steam-heated apartments in the wintertime. You can increase humidity by spraying plants with a fine mist of water once or twice a day or by growing together many plants so they create their own humidity. (A small, inexpensive space humidifier will also provide a fine mist of moisture for plants, but

I have never found one necessary.) I have 200 plants in my garden room, which has a high humidity of about 60 percent. Not only do the plants enjoy it, but so do I—high humidity does wonders for sinus problems! So if at all possible, grow your plants in one area. Plants in rooms with normally high humidity, such as the kitchen, where cooking provides some excess humidity, and the bathroom, with its steam from the shower or tub, will fare better than plants in other rooms.

ROUTINE CARE

Taking care of your solution garden is much less work than you think. There is no repotting, no weeding, and generally little worry about insects. But you must always observe plants. Keep the garden free of dirt and debris. Dutifully check the aggregate regularly to see that it is properly moist. As mentioned in the previous sections, make sure plants are getting enough light, air circulation, and humidity.

If you think you are following all good rules of soil-less gardening, but plants look wilted or are not growing well, light may be inadequate. Symptoms will be weak stems, pale leaves, or stunted growth (small leaves). Move the garden to another location. On the other hand, plants may be getting too much light; again, move the garden. Sometimes relocating the garden a few inches one way or another can result in an amazing difference in plant growth. The plants may have been in a draft or a situation where night temperatures dropped too radically rather than gradually, causing leaves to fall.

Overwatering can be a major problem, causing leaves to fall, droop, or turn yellow. Letting water sit in the container, rather than opening drainage holes regularly, can also cause leaves to drop or become yellow. (But note that leaves can fall if the aggregate does not get enough water.)

Avoid applying too much nutrient solution. This can cause

brown tips on leaves and rotted stems. Too little feeding can stunt leaf growth or cause leaves to droop and become yellow. Sun scald can spot leaves or turn them black; water dropping on foliage can also spot leaves, and frost can blacken leaves.

In caring for your solution gardens keep in mind the following factors (observance is nine-tenths of the battle in growing healthy plants):

1. The appearance of the plant itself. Is it erect and perky or wan and wilted?

2. The condition of the growing medium, including moisture content. Be alert for waterlogging or excessive drying out of the medium.

3. Be sure the container itself is functioning properly, that is, drainage holes are securely corked and aeration is good.

4. Watch the environmental conditions of light, temperature, humidity, and air circulation.

5. Observe daily rate of plant growth; if it is slow, there is something amiss. Nutrient solution may be too strong or too weak.

6. Keep watch for insect damage: eaten leaves, wilted stems.

INSECT PROBLEMS

If daily care has been maintained but plants still fail, insects might be at work. Bugs may be introduced through other plants potted in soil or from the roots of prestarted plants you have sown. The most common insects, recognizable on sight, include aphids, mealybugs, red spider mites (tiny, but discernible), scale, thrips, and whiteflies.

This plant is infested with mealybugs; note that the insects gather at leaf axils. Immediate action must be taken to save this coleus. (Photo by author)

This lipstick vine foliage shows signs of several insects: mealybug on underside of leaf and evidence of a snail or slug that ate leaf edges above. (Photo by Matthew Barr)

None of these insects are serious contenders if they are caught before they get a foothold, so the first step to healthy plants is observation. As you water plants, observe and look at and under leaves and stems for signs of crawly things.

If caught early, few insects are really a problem; you can use old-fashioned nonchemical methods of eliminating the pests (described later), or use some of the newer and relatively safe chemical preventatives as described in the following list.

How to Control Insects Chemically

INSECT	DESCRIPTION; DAMAGE	CONTROL
Aphid	Green, black, red, or pink insect, especially on new growth; sticky, shiny leaves, often cupped; sooty mold; plants stunted	Spray with Malathion or nicotine; apply a systemic.
Mealybug	White cottony clusters in stem and leaf axils; undersized foliage; spindly growth	Spray with Malathion; discard plant if heavily infested.
Red Spider Mite	Make fine webs at leaf and stem axils and underneath; leaves mottled, turning gray or brown and crumbly	Spray with Dimite.
Scale	Insect with hard or soft shell (not to be confused with seed cases on underside of fern fronds), make clusters of little brown, gray, or white lumps; plant loses vigor	Spray with Malathion or nicotine.
Thrips	Almost invisible yellow, brown, or black sucking insect; leaves deformed, streaked, or silvery with dark specks	Spray with Malathion.
Whitefly	Swarming "moth"; sooty deposits; leaves stippled or yellowing	Spray with Malathion.

Fungus disease has practically ruined this plant and there is little that can be done to save it. (Photo by Matthew Barr)

Aphids and mealybugs have infested this popular house plant, Kangaroo vine. Immediate action with chemical preventatives can save the plant. (Photo by Matthew Barr)

Nonchemical Home Remedies

If you are averse to using chemicals at home, some of the old-fashioned remedies work well to keep down insects in your solution garden. If you have a few plants, these methods are far better than using poisons indoors. Repeated applications will be necessary with most home remedies, but eventually the insects will be thwarted. Here are some ways to combat pests without resorting to chemicals:

1. *Hand picking.* This is hardly pleasant, but it can be done with a toothpick or toothbrush.

2. *Soap and water.* Use a solution of ½ pound of laundry soap (not detergent) and water to eliminate insects such as aphids and mealybugs.

3. *Alcohol.* Dip a cotton swab into alcohol and place it directly on the insect. Helps deter aphids and mealybugs.

4. *Tobacco.* Old tobacco from cigarette butts can be soaked in water for several days; then use the solution on a cotton swab to get rid of scale and red spider.

5. *Water spray.* This simple means of plant protection goes a long way in eliminating insect eggs. Spray directly on leaf axils and plant stems.

6. *Wipe leaves.* Keep leaves free from dust and dirt and thus eliminate bacteria spores that can cause plant harm.

PLANT DISEASES

Plant diseases like crown rot, botrytis, and fungus infections are generally caused by overwatering and gray days, lack of ven-

A mixture of laundry soap and water will help deter aphids and save this geranium. The best method is to dunk the entire plant in the bucket of solution and then douse with clear water. (Photo by Joyce R. Wilson)

tilation, and crowding. You will have to resort to chemical warfare, using products like Semesan and Captan. Use as directed on the package, and keep all chemicals out of the reach of children and pets.

Occasionally the surface of the aggregate may turn a light shade of green. This is no cause for alarm; it simply indicates some algae present in the aggregate. Algae conditions occur when there is too much moisture and too much bright sun. Check this problem by watering occasionally with a solution of 0.5 of a gram of copper sulfate dissolved in 2 gallons of water (available at pharmacies).

SIX

House Plants in Soil-less Gardens

House plants in gravel or pebbles in ornamental containers are attractive and a unique way to have greenery indoors. They are easy to grow and you can have house plants all year with little trouble. There is little worry about over- or underwatering, and there are a number of excellent plants to add beauty to the home scene whether on table or desk or at windows.

Seek unusual containers for your house plant solution gardens. Use glass vases or similar decorative arrangements to really put the accent on beauty.

Some house plants excel as water subjects more than others; in fact, they grow better in water than in soil. For example, if *Philodendron cordatum* is grown in soil, it invariably produces smaller leaves as the plant grows larger, which is hardly a pleasant sight. But in water solutions leaves will continue to grow normal size.

Using plants to decorate the home is popular these days and gardens in gravel suit indoor interiors perfectly, especially when plants are in simple glass containers and ornamental bowls, on tabletops or hanging. Hanging gardens are infinitely charming. At eye level plants are easily seen and add great flair to a room.

If light is limited in your home or apartment, and often it is, you can still grow plants by using artificial light. Soil-less gardening is especially suited to this kind of plant growing—the more nutrients plants have, the more light they need to assimilate the food, and artificial light (when you do not have to depend on the weather) provides light all the time.

GLASS CONTAINERS

Whenever possible I use glass containers for decorative solution gardens because filled with gravel and plants they are handsome. The plant in a clay pot is certainly fine, and I do grow many plants this way, but for something special glass is the answer. It is elegant in appearance, comes in a variety of shapes and sizes, is easy to clean, and is generally inexpensive.

Inexpensive chemical glassware (beakers or flasks) is one of my favorite types of containers. The designs are pleasing, varying from triangular to cylindrical to the standard test tube shapes. However, the glass is thin, so drilling holes in them is a tricky business. It is best to use chemical glassware containers without drainage holes and refill solutions every week. (Or have holes drilled, but at your responsibility, at glass stores.) Call your local chemical glassware supplier in yellow pages of phone book for containers.

Clear or colored wine bottles are ideal for solution gardens too because you can cut them with a bottle cutting kit. Wine bottles come in many sizes and shapes and can be used very effectively indoors as containers for many house plants. Here is a list of some of the house plants you can try in your solution gardens:

Aglaonema commutatum (Chinese evergreen). Lush, low-growing water-type plant; dark green leaves marked with silver.

A. pictum. A lovely dwarf Aglaonema; dark green, silver-spotted, velvety leaves.

Aspidistra elatior (cast-iron plant). Large dark green leaves. Handsome plant.

Avocado. One of the very popular indoor plants; grows easily in plain water; nutrients needed after planting in gravel.

Cissus rhombifolia (grape ivy). A popular trailing plant; scalloped green leaves. Grows quickly in water.

Cordyline terminalis (ti-plant). A favorite with dark green leaves lined with red. Grows easily in nutrient solutions with little care.

Cyperus alternifolius. An excellent true water plant; tall stems crowned with grassy tufts of leaves.

Dieffenbachia amoena. Heavy-textured green and white foliage on trunklike stems. Needs good support, use deep gravel bed.

D. splendens. Grows well in water. Velvety green leaves with small white dots.

Dracaena deremis werneckii. A handsome plant that does well in nutrient growing.

Pandanus veitchii. A superlative water plant; sword-shaped green and white leaves. Grows robustly in water solution.

Peperomia glomerata. Another true water plant, handsome and easy to grow; pale green, oval-shaped leaves and branching habit.

P. obtusifolia. Easily grown; fleshy, oval, green leaves.

Philodendron cordatum. Heart-shaped shiny green leaves; grows rapidly.

P. sodiroi. A graceful, lovely plant; large, heart-shaped, dark green leaves on tall stems.

Rhoeo discolor (Moses-in-a-boat). Fine rosette-type plant; colorful purple-red leaves.

Scindapsus aureus (Pothos). Smooth green leaves splashed with yellow; many handsome varieties available.

Sweet Potato. This one needs no introduction. Grows quickly in plain water.

Spathiphyllum clevelandii. This fine Aroid likes water culture; long and broad dark green leaves and rosette growth.

Other house plants to try include *Acorus gramineus* (sweet flag), *Nerium oleander* (oleander), *Tolmiea menziesii* (piggy-back plant), and *Sansevierias* (mother-in-law plant or snake plant).

Aglaonema commutatum

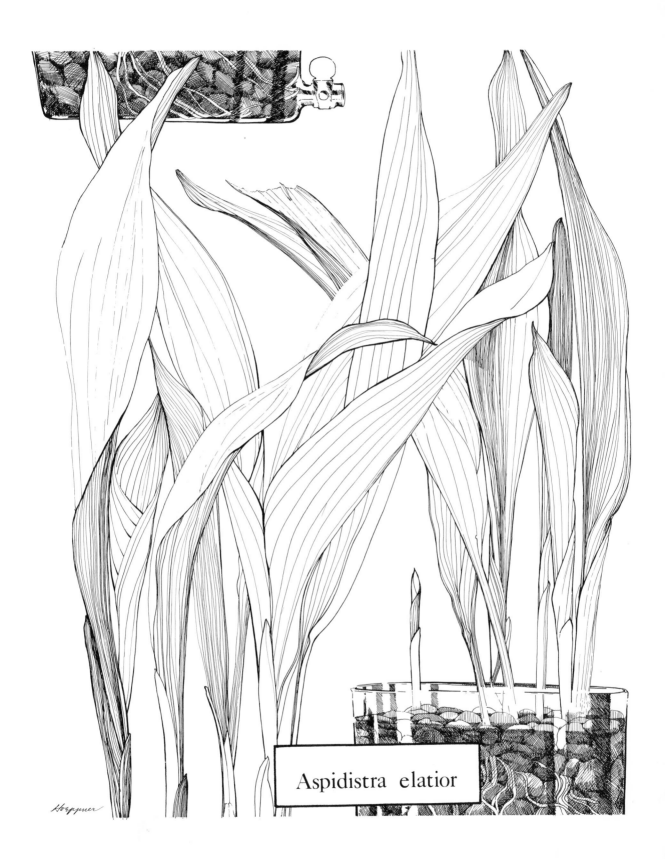

Aspidistra elatior

Avocado

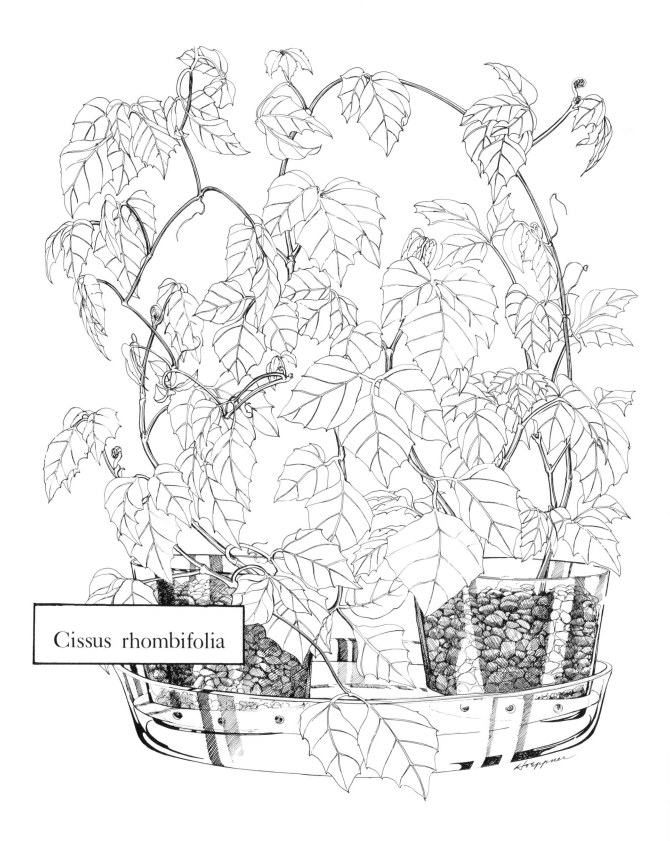

Cissus rhombifolia

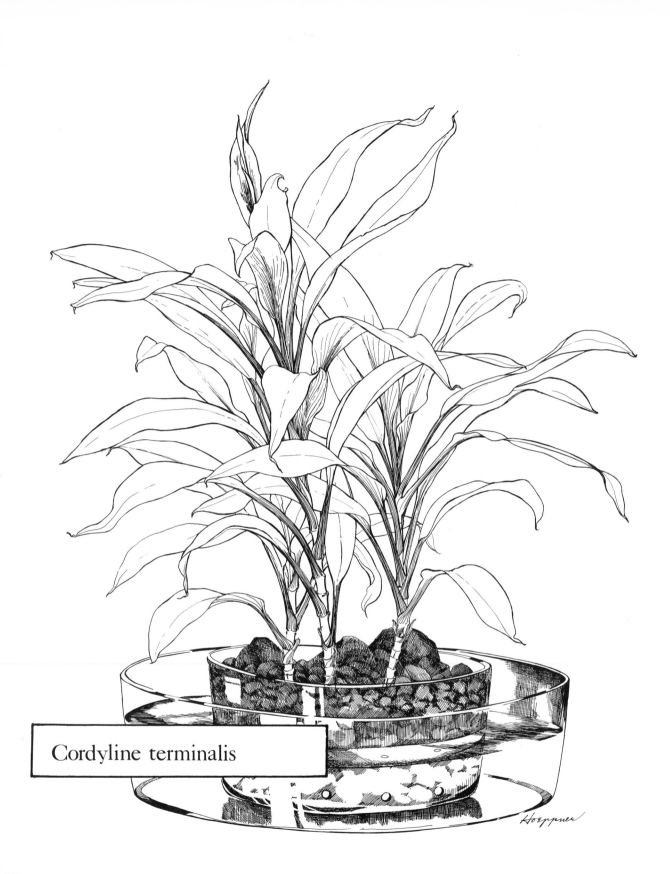

Cordyline terminalis

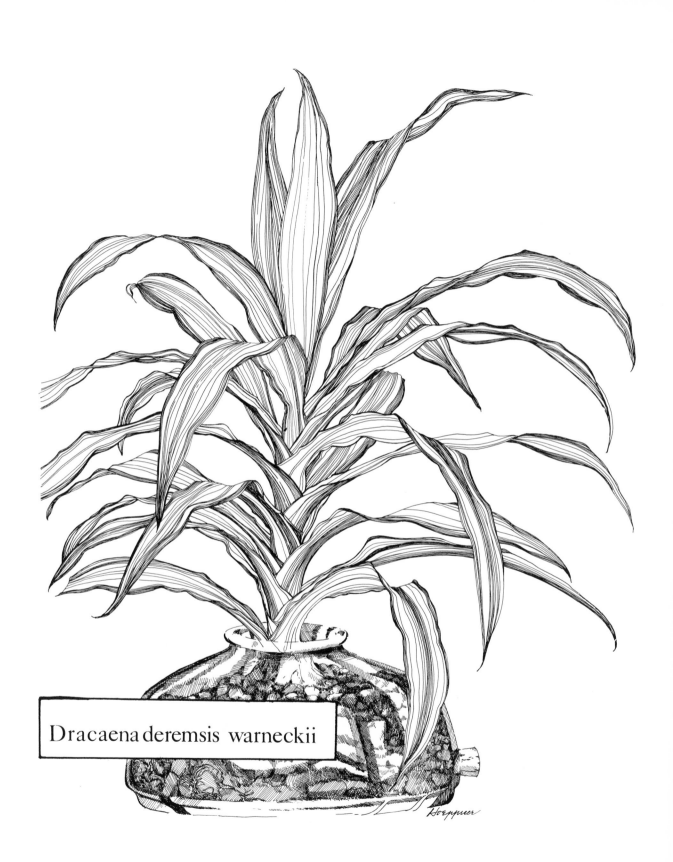

Dracaena deremsis warneckii

Sweet potato (Ipomoea)

HANGING PLANTS

Today there are many containers with hanging devices to use as pots for hanging gardens. I have seen green-colored, 6-inch rounded containers that are very suitable for gravel gardens, and some of the clear vessels (often used as hanging terrariums) are also fine indoors. Acrylic and plastic containers of many shapes are available, or, as previously mentioned, use bottles or jugs cut in half, and fashion supports from macramé slings. You can devise a number of gardens by using your imagination—supplies are at nurseries or plant stores. In any case, be sure you have adequate hardware supporting the garden, that is, sturdy ceiling hooks and chains.

Thick glass containers can be drilled easily for drainage holes at your local glass store. Acrylic too can be drilled, but you can do this yourself. However, some other types of plastics will crack if drilled.

Hang plants at eye level, neither too high, where they will seem out of place, nor too low, where they will impede traffic. No one wants to get hit in the head by a container.

Trailing Plants

Here are a few of the many fine trailing plants that can be grown in gravel and water solutions to decorate your home or apartment. None are difficult to grow, most are easy:

Abutilon hybridum (flowering maple). Scalloped bright green leaves and fine paper-thin flowers of orange, yellow, or red. Plants tend to get leggy so pinch young shoots to get bushy growth. Keep in sunny location.

Acorus gramineus (miniature flag). Not really a true trailer but does so well in water solutions it is included here. Plants have emerald-green tufted leaves and several plants to an aqua garden make a lovely display. Grow in bright light; no sun.

Aesychnanthus lobbianus (lipstick vine). With dark green leathery leaves closely set on stems, the lipstick vine bears bright red tubular flowers. The color combination of green and red is especially effective with white gravel. Plants need a bright location and frequent misting with clear water.

Alocasia amazonica. This is not a trailing plant but has exquisite leaves—green veined with white. Alocasia does very well in water solutions and needs a shady place. If you cannot find this specific species, any of the others in the family are worth space.

Begonia limminghe. One of the most handsome pendent growing begonias; needs some sun and warmth (75°F). Becomes an impressive large plant in a few years. Another excellent basket begonia is *B. foliosa* with tiny leaves, often called the fernleaf begonia.

Beloperone guttata (shrimp plant). An old favorite with deep green leaves and paper-thin colorful bracts. Prune back leggy growth in late summer to keep the plant handsome. Needs some bright light.

Bougainvillea 'Barbara Karst'. An overlooked vine that does well indoors in aqua gardens and can make quite a display with bright red bracts. Must have all the sun it can get.

Bromelia balanse (volcano plant). This fine bromeliad adapts to basket growing easily. It has spiny dark green leaves in rosette form. Start with one mature plant; eventually it will produce dozens of offshoots, making quite a showpiece. Needs sun.

Campanula fragilis (bellflower). A small, charming plant with tiny green leaves and fine star-shaped blue flowers. Needs good sun to bear flowers. Somewhat difficult but worth a try.

Chlorophytum comosum (spider plant). Grassy yellow and green leaves. Easily grown.

Cissus antarctica (kangaroo vine). Grows like a weed in water solutions. The plant has lovely dark green scalloped leaves and needs a somewhat shady location.

Fittonia vershcaffelti. A low dense creeper with soft green leaves veined red or white. Can be a handsome plant with ample heat (80°F) and humidity.

Gynura aurantica (velvet plant). A popular ornamental with purple leaves. Give sun and good humidity. Very colorful but requires some pampering.

Hedera helix (ivy). A popular plant with small scalloped bright green leaves. Observe leaves frequently; red spider often attacks foliage. Place ivy in a shady and cool situation.

Impatiens hybrids. Don't miss these fine plants for seasonal color. Improved varieties have dark green leaves and dark red flowers. Need bright light.

Lantana montevidensis. A fine flowering plant with lavender flowers on and off throughout the year. Stellar in white gravel aqua gardens. Give bright light.

Philodendron. A large group of mostly vining plants. Most need bright light. Heart-shaped leaves and easy growing make them a favorite with gardeners. Try *P. oxycardium, P. hastatum,* and *P. sodiroi.*

Plechtranthus oertendahii (Swedish ivy). An easy-to-grow plant with lovely bright green scalloped leaves. Likes bright light.

Rhipsalis paradoxa (mistletoe cactus). A spineless cactus with pendent growth and handsome colorful berries in winter. Grows easily in most situations.

Rhaphidophora aureus. An overlooked plant with handsome scalloped leaves. Does well in water.

Saxifraga sarmentosa (strawberry geranium). Neither a strawberry nor a geranium but still a good indoor plant. Leaves are geranium-shaped with strawberry coloring. Needs bright light.

Scindapsus aureus (ivy-arum). With smooth dark green leaves splashed with yellow or white, this is an excellent trailer for aqua gardening. Needs only bright light to prosper.

Syngonium podophyllum (arrow-head). An excellent water plant, handsome arrow-shaped leaves.

Tradescantia fluminensis (wandering Jew). Fast-growing plant with oval leaves in cream-and-green or plain green. Grows in shade or sun.

Zebrina pendula (wandering Jew). Pretty trailing silver-and-purple-leaved plants, Zebrinas are ideal for basket growing. Many new varieties available.

Generally the perimeter of the room and near windows are the best places for hanging containers because they can be seen easily and yet be out of the way of traffic.

Acorus gramineus variegatus

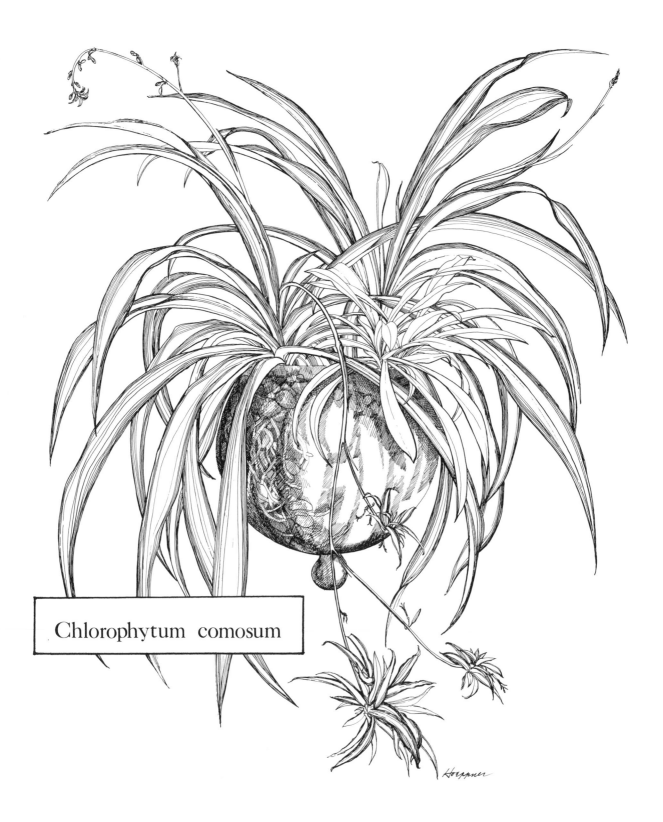

Chlorophytum comosum

Cissus antarctica

Philodendron oxycardium

Rhaphidophora aurea

Syngonium podophyllum

Tradescantia fluminensis

GRAVEL AND SAND GARDENS

You can "sculpt" your own unique plant creation with some gravel and sand and any glass jar or vessel; the arrangement of various colored, layered material is delightful. To start, you will need a clear (glass or plastic) vase, various grades of gravel and colored sand (if not available at Woolworths, try building supply yards), and plants.

Put layers of gravel or colored sand in the glass container. You can put in 1 level inch of this and 2 level inches of that, but a wavy pattern is best for a more pleasing arrangement. Blend colors to your taste; use fine- and large-grained gravel. Once you have created your arrangement, embed the plants in the top layer.

Now the container must be filled with water, and this involves patience and extreme care. Fill the container with water as you would an aquarium: set stiff cardboard inside the glass, along the walls, and dribble water into the vase. Do it slowly and with a steady hand because if you pour too fast, you will ruin and disturb the design. As water infiltrates the sand arrangement, the colors take on life and glisten. Fill the container to within 1 inch of the top. By the way, it is best to set up the textured garden right where you want it rather than trying to move it later to another place. A container filled with sand and water can weigh quite a bit, so moving it can be a problem.

As the roots of the plant take hold in the top layer of sand or gravel, they will infiltrate through the textured picture you have created, adding interesting effects and designs. Ultimately you will have a natural picture that is distinctive and unique. Experience is the best teacher, and it does take a deft hand and good color sense to create a pleasing picture.

Any plant previously mentioned can be used for gravel-and-sand gardens.

ARTIFICIAL LIGHT

Many home gardeners have found artificial light a satisfactory way of supplying light to indoor plants when natural light is lacking. As with soil-less gardening, where you can control the nutrients given a plant and thus have plants growing all year, plants under artificial light can be grown all year long too, which is a definite plus in having strong, healthy, and lush plants.

There are many kinds of artificial light, but the most commonly used types are fluorescent and incandescent. The visible spectrum has colors ranging from red to violet; research indicates that plants need blue, red, and far-red to produce good growth. Blue enables plants to manufacture carbohydrates, and red controls how they take up nutrients and affects the plants' response to the relative length of light and darkness. Far-red rays work in tandem with red in many ways: It controls stem length, seed germination, and leaf size by reversing or nullifying the action of red rays.

Plants grow best when they have sufficient levels of blue/red light, which is standard in fluorescent tubes, and far-red light, which is in incandescent (reading) bulbs. Some researchers claim that the rest of the spectrum is necessary for optimum growth, but this has not yet been proved.

Fluorescent lamps are available in many wattages and temperature characteristics, under such trade names such as Cool White, Daylight, Warm White, Natural White, and Soft White. Besides these standard fluorescent lamps, there are also lamps solely designed for plant growth, such as Gro-Lux by Sylvania Lighting Company, Plant Gro by Westinghouse Electric Company, and Vitima by Durolite Electric Company. The choice of lamps is arbitrary; some people use those made solely for plant growth, but others use standard fluorescent lamps such as Cool White, which is my choice. Cool White provides necessary blue and red for plant growth, whereas some lamps in the standard category—daylight, for example—are high in blue but low in red. Fluorescent lamps come in 24, 40, or 72 watts in a number of lengths, with 40-inch the most popular.

Generally, but not always, fluorescent lights are used with incandescent lamps. I use two 8-watt incandescent lamps to every 80 watts of fluorescent, which has worked well for most of my house plants.

Incandescent lamps also come in many wattages and types. A plant grown only under incandescent light, such as a 60-watt reading lamp, left on about 12 hours a day, will grow better than a plant not under lights. The main objection to incandescent light is that it gives off heat and thus can be too hot or drying for plants. However, if the plant is kept a reasonable distance from the lamp, 24 to 36 inches, this does not occur. Recently a new incandescent Plant Gro light appeared. This supposedly has a sufficient blue and red ratio so that additional fluorescent light is not needed. This bulb fits conveniently into any porcelain socket lamp. I do grow some plants under this bulb, but the majority are under a combination of fluorescent and incandescent light, which is what I recommend.

Just how much artificial fluorescent light you can give your plants must be tempered by common sense and, to some degree, experiment. Here are four general rules: (1) For germinating seeds and cuttings, use 10 lamp watts per square foot of growing area; (2) for house plants and vegetables, use 20 lamp watts per square foot of growing area; (3) keep plants 3 to 5 inches from light source; (4) a good normal light period for foliage plants is 12 to 14 hours daily; for flowering plants and vegetables, have lights on 16 to 18 hours daily. For aqua gardens using artificial light try some of these plants:

Begonias: A large group including Rex begonias, Angel-wings, hirsute types, and rhizomatus plants. Most do satisfactorily with 12 to 14 hours of artificial light. B. 'Alleyri' and B. 'Alto Scharff' excel in the hirsute group. B. 'Argentea Guttata' and B. 'Pink

Spot Lucerne' excellent as typical angel-wing types, and in the rhizomatous category try B. 'Crestabruchi' or B. 'Maphil'.

Bromeliads: These indestructible plants grow almost in any situation and are really care-free indoor subjects. Here are some of the smaller specimens for aqua gardening:

Aechmea fasciata. Tufted blue and pink flower heads in spring; banded leaves.

A. racinae. Dark green leaves; red berries.

Neoregelia carolinae. Dark green leaves tipped with red.

Vriesea splendens. The flaming sword plant with rosette growth and orange "swords" on erect stems.

Geraniums: Another large group of fine indoor plants including small or large plants. Most need coolness (60°F) and 14 to 18 hours of artificial light per day. Here are some of the better miniatures for growing in aqua gardens:

'Bumble Bee'. Dark green leaves; red flowers. 'Fairy Princess'. Dark leaves; creamy pink blooms. 'Imp'. Dark foliage; salmon pink flowers. 'Liliput Lemon'. Lemon-scented waxy leaves. 'Polaris'. Dark green foliage'; pink edged flowers. 'Tangerine'. Free blooming salmon. 'Tweedledee'. Scalloped leaves; salmon flowers.

Gesneriads: Popular plants including Aesychnanthus, Columnea, Kohleria, Hypocyrta, Episcia, Rechsteinaria, Saintpaulia (African violets), and Smithianthas.

Keep gesneriads about 78°F by day and 10 to 15 degrees less at night. Provide good ventilation and provide 14 to 16 hours of artificial light daily.

Aeschynanthus lobbianus. Fine dark green leaves, red flowers.

Columnea arguta. Trailing vine with pointed leaves; red blooms.

Episcia 'Yellow Topaz'. Green foliage; yellow flowers.

Kohleria amabilis. Velvety green leaves; pink flowers.

Rechsteinaria leucotricha. Large leaves; coral blooms.

Saintpaulia. Many, many varieties; most with oval leaves and blue or lavender flowers.

Smithiantha multiflora. Soft hairy plant; white flowers.

Other plants such as Marantas and Calatheas and Philo-dendrons can also be grown under lights with very satisfactory results.

GROWING METHODS

It is possible to grow house plants in water without solutions, but plants will last longer if you use the water solution. Apply the solutions mentioned in Chapter 4 about twice a week. Drain away excess solution before applying the new mixture, and keep the aggregate moist. If you do decide to grow plants in clear water only, add some charcoal chips to keep water sweet, replace evaporated water when necessary, and periodically replace the water with fresh water.

Whether you grow plants in water only or with solution, keep plants in a bright but not sunny place. As mentioned, direct sun can do more harm than good; the majority of house plants will do just fine in bright light only. Maintain a daytime temperature of 75°F, 65°F or 60°F by night. Mist plant foliage occasionally to keep it in good health, and a few times a year wipe foliage with a damp cloth to eliminate dust and any insect eggs that may have formed. Do *not* ever use leaf-shining preparations because they can clog leaf pores. Keep house plants out of drafts and away from doors that are frequently being opened or closed.

No matter what kind of container you use for soil-less gardening—boxes, trays, bins, decorative housings—be sure it has drainage holes and be sure you have a supply of stoppers and corks to fit the holes to keep the nutrients within the aggregate. An exception would be the sand-and-gravel decorative gardens which should not be disturbed and these containers need no drainage holes.

WHERE TO PUT GARDENS

The location of your indoor garden depends mostly on the size and kind of container. Decorative containers can go almost any place because they are handsome. More utilitarian housings such as trays and bins look better in a kitchen or basement. Plants like Crotons and Sansevierias have to be in large trays so of course need larger spaces: on window ledges perhaps.

No matter where you put the garden, be sure the container has a suitable saucer or some dish or device to catch moisture seepage that can stain furniture tops. Cork mats or wooden pedestals are fine. Terra cotta saucers and trays are good, although often they need a protective coating because they are porous and thus water will seep through in time.

SEVEN

Sowing Seed: Annuals, Perennials, House Plants, Vegetables

Starting your own plants from seeds (annuals and perennials, house plants, and vegetables) is becoming more popular these days because of the rising cost of plants. Besides saving you money, growing from seeds makes good sense because you can have the plants you want rather than what is available. With soil-less gardening, seed sowing is so easy that even a child can do it. No special apparatus or equipment is needed, and once seeds are sown, all you have to do is keep the aggregate moist with necessary nutrients. When the seedlings are a few inches high, they can be transplanted into single water-solution containers. When you are sowing seed in soil there is always the danger of overwatering and soil contaminants to thwart plant growth. Not so in water gardening—the porous and open texture of the aggregate helps prevent waterlogged conditions, and the gravel or sand is, of course, sterile.

As previously mentioned, you can grow all kinds of plants from seed—vegetables, house plants, flowers. Just what you grow depends on the space you have and what you particularly want. A few home-grown vegetables are always welcome, and your own house plants are indeed a satisfaction, let alone the savings involved!

HOW TO START

For a propagating case all you need is a suitable container, that is, any household throwaway item like plastic cartons or the aluminum pans frozen rolls come in. You can also use casseroles or terra cotta pots, or make a seed-sowing case from a wooden

This photo shows a seed setup: gravel and vermiculite at right, casserole for the medium and seeds at left, and cover to assure humidity for seeds in center. (Photo by author)

grocery box. No matter what you use, be sure it has drainage holes in the bottom.

Fill the container with about 2 to 3 inches of aggregate—small pea-sized gravel has worked well for me. (Standard seed starting media sold under various trade names is also satisfactory for starting seeds.) Moisten the medium with plain water. Now insert seeds. Embed large seeds about ⅓ inch deep in the aggregate (make holes with a pencil), and then cover them. For fine seeds, remove a little aggregate from the surface, put the seeds in place, and then replace the aggregate. Once the seeds are in place, apply solution evenly over the aggregate, and smooth down the aggregate.

If you prefer to use prestarted plants, be sure to wash away all soil from the roots (hold them under running water). Then make small holes in the aggregate, equally spaced, and drop in the plants; rake back the growing medium around them. The plants should not wobble, so firm stones around the collar.

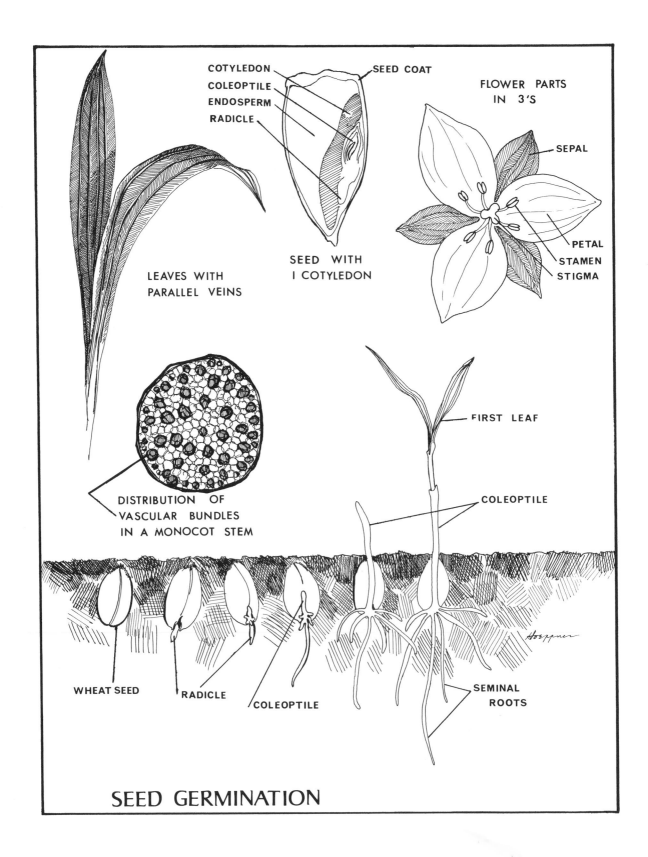

COTYLEDON
COLEOPTILE
ENDOSPERM
RADICLE

SEED COAT

FLOWER PARTS
IN 3'S

SEPAL

PETAL
STAMEN
STIGMA

LEAVES WITH
PARALLEL VEINS

SEED WITH
I COTYLEDON

FIRST LEAF

COLEOPTILE

DISTRIBUTION OF
VASCULAR BUNDLES
IN A MONOCOT STEM

WHEAT SEED

RADICLE

COLEOPTILE

SEMINAL
ROOTS

SEED GERMINATION

Seed Starting Techniques

One good method for sowing seeds is to use an azalea pot (at suppliers) about 8 inches in diameter. Fill it with gravel or sand, wet the aggregate, and be sure the hole is stopped up. Then put a 2- or 3-inch pot into the center of the aggregate to a depth of about 1 inch from the bottom. Plant the seeds in the perimeter of the 8-inch pot. Water the seeds by placing water in the empty small pot in the center. When the seedlings have germinated apply nutrient solution, pouring it gently around the seedlings.

When you see fresh green growth, start thinning out weaklings so the other plants will have space to grow. When seedlings are a few inches high, they can be removed with a blunt-edged stick and replanted in single aqua gardens.

You can also start seed in Jiffy Pellets (these are peat moss wafers about ½ inch thick). Place two or three seeds to each wafer

Seed starting is simple in this simple arrangement. Seed is embedded in the medium of the large pot; water is poured when necessary into center of small pot to supply moisture. (Photo by Jack Barnick)

Jiffy Pellets are excellent for starting seed. The full size "pot" with a petunia in it is ready to be planted, pot and all, in the aqua garden. (Photo courtesy Jiffy Pot Co. of America)

and put the wafers in a watertight pan or tray. Keep adding water to the bottom of the tray; moisture is drawn up from the bottom to nourish the seed. When seedlings germinate and growth is about 2 inches tall insert the pot and seedling in gravel in the solution garden. When it is time to transplant the seedling into its permanent growing area gently pull up the whole pellet with roots from the gravel. Generally, the root ball will stay intact and not mess up the hydroponic unit.

When starting seeds use enough to assure a good yield. Seeds are not overly expensive so use them freely. Thus, if some seeds do not germinate, others will and the odds are in your favor.

Maintaining Seeds

Maintain the seeds in a continually damp condition, never too wet, never too dry; they should never be waterlogged. Every few days remove the plugs in the drainage holes for a short time —about 1 hour—to allow unused water or solution inside the bot-

Commercial suppliers sell complete pellet seed setups for starting plants and these can certainly be used to get plantlets ready for aqua gardens. (Photo courtesy Park Seed Co.)

tom of the container to seep out into trays or saucers. (Always remember to replace plugs in drainage holes before making the next application of nutrient solution.) Generally, every-other-day applications of nutrients are all that is needed. Keep seed trays in a warm (78°F), bright (but not sunny) place.

Never overwater with the nutrient solution because this prevents aeration, and without air moving through the root zone, plants may die. Once every 2 weeks leach plants of excess nutrients: spray plain water on the aggregate surface. To germinate, seeds must have plenty of moisture (humidity 50 to 70 percent), air, proper temperatures (75°F by day, 65°F by night), and bright but not sunny light. When the seedlings sprout, they will need brighter light and some sunshine. In sunny light seedlings grow at night, so the night temperature should be lower than the day temperature. The best way to maintain humidity is to use the tent method: Cover the container with a Baggie, propping up the bag with thin pieces of wood.

When seeds have germinated (time varies with the plant being grown, from 10 days to many weeks), and first true leaves (second set of leaves) are visible, remove weaker seedlings in each group and discard them. This permits the stronger plants to develop. When seedlings are a few inches high, each one can be removed and put into individual water garden containers—a clay pot perhaps (if it is a house plant), a larger planter if you are growing vegetables. Increase light now for the young plants (most should have some sun), and keep the aggregate in the container moist, never soggy and never dry. Once plants are in permanent containers, grow them by normal aqua gardening techniques.

GARDEN FLOWERS

Here are some (but not all) garden flowers (annuals and perennials) you can grow from seeds. All sorts can be grown, depending on the uses you have for the plants and the plants you personally like. (Following this general list are tables of specific annuals and perennials.)

Asters: Asters come in many shapes and sizes and forms and colors. Can be started from seed or prestarted plants that are available at nurseries in seasonal times. Give Asters some shading against direct sun, and keep temperatures as even as possible. Give plenty of nutrients to ensure a good crop of flowers.

Carnations: These plants are grown commercially by the hydroponic method. Try some on a small scale; start plants when they are available at nurseries, or start your own from seed. Keep temperatures rather cool, about 55°F.

Chrysanthemums: Chrysanthemums are available in a galaxy of different varieties and colors. Good drainage is essential, and ample light is necessary to produce a bumper crop. Keep pinching out growth tips to ensure a good yield of flowers.

Dahlias: These flowers are not as easy to grow hydroponically as most flowers because mildew is a frequent problem. Can be grown from cuttings.

Gazania: Grow plants in a coarser aggregate than other plants. Keep seeds just barely moist, never overly wet. Cuttings root easily in aggregate too.

Marigolds: Marigolds can be easily grown in hydroponic gardens. Do well with ample sun and good drainage. Many excellent varieties are available.

Nasturtiums: Certainly the easiest of all flowers to grow. Good aeration and sunlight are all that are needed. Keep gravel uniformly moist; even slight drying out will affect plants adversely.

Pansies: These fanciful flowers are another easy candidate for the aqua garden. Require good drainage and plenty of nutrient solution.

Petunias: Easily grown from seed in gravel and solution. Keep medium uniformly moist, never soggy, and give plants ample sun.

Roses: Standard varieties need large containers, which might prove a problem, but some of the miniature roses can certainly be grown. Give roses cool temperatures (55°F), proper aeration, and good drainage.

Stock: One of the most popular cut flowers. Grow very well in

Chrysanthemums make a good hydroponic crop and grow well in water solution. You will need a greenhouse to grow these but they are worth a try. (Photo by Joyce R. Wilson)

Another favorite garden flower (Gazania) can be tried in the soil-less garden. (Photo by author)

aqua gardens if temperatures are kept within 70° to 75°F. Seed germinates easily. Excellent plants for the beginner to try.

Snapdragons: Another very popular cut flower. Easily started from seed in hydroponic treatment. Need generous feedings and good light to succeed.

Sweet Peas: Keep the aggregate cool and moist, and sow seed about ½ inch deep in gravel or sand. Keep the aggregate evenly moist; never soggy, never too dry. Coolness is the key to success, so try temperatures of 55°F to 60°F once seeds have germinated.

Zinnias: These lovely flowers need only ample nutrient solution and good light to succeed in the aqua garden.

TABLE OF ANNUALS AND PERENNIALS
*Annuals

BOTANICAL AND COMMON NAMES	OPTIMUM TEMPERATURE FOR SEED GERMINATION	WEEKS REQUIRED FOR SEEDS TO GERMINATE
*Antirrhinum majus (snapdragon)	60°–65°F	1–2
Aster (michaelmas daisy)	68°–70°F	2–3
*Calendula officinalis (pot marigold)	68°–70°F	2–3
*Callistephus chinensis (China aster)	68°F	2–3
Campanula carpatica (Carpathian harebell)	68°–86°F	2–3
*Chrysanthemum (many kinds)	68°–70°F	2–4
Coreopsis	68°–70°F	2–4
*Delphinium ajacis (larkspur)	60°–65°F	2–3
Dianthus (pinks)	68°–75°F	2–3
*Dimorphotheca (Cape marigold)	68°–70°F	2–3
*Gazania	68°–72°F	2–3
Helenium autumnale (sneezeweed)	68°F	1–2
Lathyrus latifolius (pea vine)	68°–86°F	2–3
*Mathiola incana (stock)	54°–90°F	2
*Mirabilis (four-o-clock)	68°–86°F	1–2
Myosotis (forget-me-not)	68°F	2–3

BOTANICAL AND COMMON NAMES	OPTIMUM TEMPERATURE FOR SEED GERMINATION	WEEKS REQUIRED FOR SEEDS TO GERMINATE
*Petunia (many kinds)	68°–70°F (some varieties need higher temperatures)	2–3
Pyrethrum (painted daisy)	68°–76°F	2–3
Rudbeckia (coneflower)	70°–86°F	2–3
*Tagetes (marigold)	68°–86°F	1–2
Viola cornuta	55°–90°F	2–3
Zinnia elegans (zinnia)	68°–86°F	1–2

HOUSE PLANTS

You can start your own house plants from seed using the methods previously described for annuals and perennials. Because house plants are expensive today it makes good sense to grow your own plants. You can buy packaged seed from suppliers or if you prefer, you can start seedlings purchased from nurseries. I have had considerable success buying 2-inch potted seedlings of all kinds of house plants—Dracaena, Dizygotheca, Philodendron. These are in the terrarium plant section at suppliers (although they are not true miniature plants). I then transfer these plants to the solution garden. To do this remove the tiny plant from the pot, wash away all soil, and insert into the aggregate. Then grow the plants normally as you would any other plant. When they are 6 to 8 inches tall they are ready for permanent planting in decorative soil-less gardens.

Germination time for house plant seed varies with the plant you are growing, but most germinate in 10 to 30 days in a temperature of 70° to 80°F. Constant warmth and uniform moisture are necessary. Here are some of the easier house plants you might want to start from seed:

Begonias: Many types including fibrous, rhizomatous, hirsute, and angel-wings. Begonia seed is very fine, so scatter on top of growing medium. Provide warmth (78°F); germination is 7 to 20 days depending on variety used.

Cacti and Succulents: These fine indoor plants are very easy to grow from seed. Some seed is very fine and should be lightly covered; others are larger and need to be imbedded a scant ¼ inch in the aggregate. Seeds will need warmth (70° to 80°F) to germinate. Some germinate in about 15 days; others in about 30 days. In this group you can grow Kleinia, Crassula, Kalanchoes, Echeverias as well as Mammilaria, Rebutias, Parodias, and so forth.

Crossandra infundibuliformis. A fine flowering plant with shiny leaves and orange blooms. Seeds germinate at about 75°F in 21 to 30 days. A fast-growing plant.

Ficus: The rubber tree and banyan tree are in this group. Do not completely cover seed; use just a light covering of aggregate. Seed germinates best at 65° to 70°F in about 20 days.

Gesneriads: This group includes a host of very fine indoor plants such as Columnea, Episcia, Rechsteinaria, Smithiantha, and the popular African violet (Saintpaulia). Plants are easily started from seed and do best with daytime temperatures of 75° to 80°F, and nighttime, about 65°F. Columneas germinate in about 20 days; Episcias, 25 to 40 days. Rechsteinarias are radical and sometimes start in 15 days, other times about 30 days. The popular African violets germinate in 20 to 30 days.

Geraniums. These fine indoor plants are relatively easy to grow from seed. Seed germinates at 65° to 70°F, taking 15 to 25 days.

Jacobinia. This fine flowering plant is easy to grow from seed and makes a fine indoor accent. Sow seed at 70° to 78°F. Germination takes about 2 weeks.

The above are only a few of the many plants you can try from seed; for more fun, experiment with your favorites. It is easy with soil-less gardening and saves a great deal of money if you are a house plant lover as I am.

CUTTINGS

Cuttings ("slips") are a convenient way of increasing plants. Take either stem or leaf cuttings (I use a razor blade). For stem cuttings, take 4-inch pieces, cutting them just below a leaf node (the little swelling in the stem), and remove the foliage from the lower 2 inches. Place the cuttings in vermiculite in a seed pan or squatty clay pot, cover the container with a Baggie, and keep the cuttings in warmth (about 78°F). For leaf cuttings, take leaves from such plants as African violets, Kalanchoes, or Rex begonias; cut across the leaf veins in several places on the underside. (Do not slice the leaves.) Then place the leaves right side up, flat, on sand or vermiculite. To be sure there is contact between the leaves and aggregate, weigh down the leaves with pebbles. To ensure good humidity, place a Baggie over the container and keep it warm. Plantlets will soon appear and use the old leaves as nourishment. When the new plants can be handled easily, move them to a permanent place in the solution garden. Leaf or stem cuttings taken in spring and summer are more apt to root than those taken in fall or winter.

When you are caring for cuttings, be sure they have ample

Cuttings also grow into big plants; this tip cutting already shows roots forming after only two weeks and is ready for separate planting. (Photo USDA)

humidity, good warmth (78°F), and light. Direct sun should not be given until plants are growing. Keep nutrient solution in the growing bin and the medium always moist, never dry. Great care must be given the plants until they are growing; after they are in their permanent housings, apply routine care.

SOWING VEGETABLE SEED

Too many people overlook the benefits of growing fresh and

tasty miniature vegetables in water solutions. To survive, most vegetables need plenty of water. Water, along with insects, is what may harm vegetables grown in soil, but this is not so in water culture. Also consider that vegetables grown in water mature more quickly than those grown in soil and generally produce far higher yields in less space! This is important to home dwellers who want a few fresh vegetables in small spaces. Finally, by growing vegetables in water you avoid the chemicals and artificial colorings commercial growers often use in their soil-grown crops.

You can grow many vegetables from seed, but cucumbers and lettuce are the easiest. However, do try spinach, radishes, beets, and beans. (Eggplant, escarole, onions, peppers, and tomatoes should be started preplanted.) Containers should be from 8 to 20 inches in diameter, depending on the plant. Climate will determine what type of vegetable you grow. Some are warm season, preferring to be planted in the spring for summer harvesting; others are cool season, those that should be planted in the summer and harvested in the late fall. Midget types can be grown on windowsills; grow standard varieties in the yard or greenhouse.

Tips
Water-grown crops need ample sun and optimum temperatures (72° to 80°F) for good harvest. Use the Baggie tent method for good humidity. Plant warm-season vegetables in April or May and harvest them in July or August, or you can get a head start by planting a few months earlier. Late July and all of August are the months in which to plant cool-season plants; harvest them in late September to the middle of November. Radishes, chard, lettuce, carrots, and beets are in this latter category.

Cabbage, Cauliflower
Cabbage and cauliflower need a very loose aggregate because they must have plenty of air at their roots. They also need plenty

Cauliflower is a welcome winter vegetable crop and can be tried in soil-less gardens. (Photo courtesy Burpee Seed Co.)

of nutrients. These plants are heavy "eaters," so drainage must be perfect. Cabbage and cauliflower require large containers, so use boxes or planters at least 18 inches by 30 inches long by 10 inches deep. You will probably need a greenhouse or at least a yard to grow these vegetables properly.

Carrots

Carrots do exceptionally well in hydroponic units as long as they have a loose aggregate. Frequently water and feed carrots because they *must* have fast growth. Use a container 10 to 12 inches in diameter, with seeds planted to a depth of ½ inch. Thin out seedlings when they are 2 inches tall and again 1 month later. Carrots grow to about 12 inches, ready for harvesting in 70 to 75 days. Try the following varieties: Baby Finger Nantes, Tiny Sweet, Nantes, and Short n' Sweet.

Cucumbers

These strong plants grow quickly in a 12-inch container with heat (85°F). Plant seeds to a depth of 1 inch, and insert stakes into the aggregate so plants can climb. Cucumbers grow to 30 inches; they can be harvested in 50 to 55 days. Good varieties are Triumph Hybrid, Patio Pick, and China Hybrid.

Lettuce

Lettuce grows quickly in soil-less gardens, preferring cool (65°F) temperatures and light. Use a rapidly draining aggregate because excess water will rot lower leaves. Plant seeds to a ½-inch depth in an 8- to 10-inch container. You can harvest plants in 30 to 40 days. The loose-head (leafy) varieties are superb: Oak Leaf, Buttercrunch, Bibb lettuce, Salad Bowl, and Tom Thumb Bibb. (By the way, the lettuces' foliage is so attractive that plants are ideal for decoration.)

Chard

Chard, which has a spinach-like flavor, is foolproof: it likes hot or cold temperatures, wetness or dryness. Plant seeds 1 inch deep in an 8- to 16-inch container (a pot or jug is good). Thin out plants when they are 10 inches tall, and remove the outer leaves. (You do not absolutely have to remove the outer leaves, but plants will produce into early winter if you do.) You can harvest chard in 75 days. Try Fordhook Giant and Lucullus varieties.

Beets

Plant beet seeds 1 to 2 inches deep in a 10- to 12-inch container.

Keep temperatures cool and plants evenly moist, in a shady spot. Water frequently. Thin plants when they are 2 inches tall, again when they reach 9 inches. Harvest beets in 50 to 60 days. Good varieties are Spring Red, Detroit Dark Red, and Ruby Queen.

Beans

Beans need warmth and much water and solution. Plant seeds 1 inch deep in an 8- to 10-inch container. Pick leaves when they are young for good flavor and growth. You can harvest beans in 50 to 55 days. Try Henderson Bush, Blue Lake Bush Bean, Sprite Bush Green Bean, Honey Gold Wax Bean, and Bush Romano Bean varieties.

Radishes

Anyone can grow radishes; you cannot fail. Plant seeds ½ inch deep in a 6- to 8-inch container. Water copiously, and avoid hot temperatures. Apply solution when the first leaves appear. Harvest in 20 to 30 days. The four good varieties are Icicle, Cherry, Champion Radish, and Bell Radish.

Squash

Squash is a member of the cucumber family and so needs heat and much water. Plant seeds 1 inch deep in a 16- to 20-inch container; put stakes into the aggregate. Thin and feed plants regularly, and harvest early and often (60 to 64 days). Varieties include Cocozelle, Early White Bush, Summer Crookneck, and Gold Nugget (all summer squash); Butternut and True Hubbard (winter squash).

Tomatoes

These are a favorite hydroponic crop and like warm conditions, some shading, and good aeration in the aggregate. Start pre-planted plants in a gravel bed. The plants require nonstop feeding and warm temperatures. Use a commercial pollinating prepara-

Beans are another favorite crop. (Photo by Burpee Seed Co.)

Squash likes plenty of food and does very well in soil-less gardening. (Photo courtesy Burpee Seed Co.)

The popular patio tomato, an easy-to-grow vegetable even for the novice.
(Photo courtesy Park Seed Co.)

tion, and keep plants staked. There are dozens of standard varieties, but for the small garden try the midget types such as Tom Thumb and Patio.

EIGHT

Greenhouse Soil-less Gardens

Greenhouses are ideal for solution gardens because in these enclosed, adequately ventilated structures you can regulate humidity, temperature, and air with little trouble. Plants in water solutions in greenhouses will grow lavishly, perhaps too fast. Also, it is possible to have tropical plants in the middle of winter and vegetables when you want them. And of course there is always the sheer satisfaction of beautiful green plants to greet you every morning.

Once greenhouses were expensive, but today a small 8- x 10-foot prefabricated unit can be constructed for about $600. This is a small investment for the many hours of pleasure the greenhouse will provide. Various manufacturers offer a gamut of structures, from lean-to (against a house wall) to free-standing units. For best results the greenhouse should face south, but I have seen lovely glass gardens on the east and west sides of the home. The main consideration is that there is easy access to the house.

GREENHOUSE CONTAINERS

Some greenhouses come with benches that can be used as planting bins, but you have to modify them for soil-less gardening. It is better to construct your own plant trays, 3 to 4 feet long and 6 inches deep. Root vegetables will need somewhat deeper containers, about 10 inches. Put drainage holes at the sides rather than at the bottom of the tray, and install a gutter to carry off excess water. Use pipes, prefabricated irrigation systems, or a hose to apply water and solution. Concrete troughs or pans can also be used if necessary.

No matter which containers you choose, have adequate supports or stands for them. If you buy a prefabricated greenhouse, you

Wooden trays or "flats" are used to start seeds here; in a greenhouse conditions are almost perfect for soil-less gardening. (Photo by Matthew Barr)

can also purchase the standard bench supports for your solution garden trays. Or build your own wood or metal structures; simple table framing may be all you need to hold the trays.

GREENHOUSE ROUTINE

Plants will grow quickly in a greenhouse with optimum conditions, so it is important to check the aggregate daily to determine if it is properly moist. As with indoor soil-less gardens, the need for nutrient solution varies with the time of year and the particular plants being grown. Other factors, such as moisture in the air, temperature, and ventilation, must be considered also. Excessive moisture in the air coupled with dark days can create rot in plants, so let the outside weather be your guide. On cloudy, dull days do not water as much, and keep ventilation at a maximum. Remember that excessive wetness will hinder proper aeration of the aggregate, and waterlogged plants soon die.

Humidity

Maintain an average humidity of 60 percent (less at night). In the winter, high humidity coupled with dark days can create a breeding ground for plant fungus and bacteria. Use a hygrometer to measure the humidity. You will have to increase the humidity if you use much artificial heat in the winter. Keep the humidity high when the days are very hot.

Routine watering will provide sufficient humidity for the plants growing together and thus allow good growth; you will *not* need expensive misters or foggers.

Temperature

Keep the greenhouse temperature at 75 to 90 degrees in the

Good light coming through translucent fiberglass panels makes plants grow lushly; humidity too is excellent in this greenhouse with a dirt floor. (Photo by Matthew Barr)

day, 65 to 80 at night. In the winter, raise the heat if nights are very cold (a few very cold nights will *not* harm plants). Sudden temperature changes can damage plants, but if you carefully regulate the opening of windows and doors, you can *gradually* lower the temperatures. On very hot days, the greenhouse can become overly hot, causing plants to lose moisture fast, so spray and mist plants with water.

Ventilation

A good circulation of air is essential for all plants because it provides relief from the sun, controls such disease problems as mildew, and ensures good humidity. The atmosphere should be buoyant and fresh, never stagnant or stale. Keep ventilation at a maximum, and even in winter, be sure some air is entering the greenhouse. Hot air rises, so provide vents at the top of the green-house to let out the hot air.

Shading

Some plants die overnight if subject to even one day of extreme heat about 100°F, and leaf temperature over 120°F immediately scorches and kills plant cells. You are going to have to provide some shading for the structure unless your greenhouse is at an east exposure (getting only morning sun).

Old-fashioned paste or whiting powder can be applied with a spray or paintbrush, but this is a bother and ugly looking. Plastic shading also looks terrible. Use movable aluminum- or wood-slatted venetian blinds or bamboo rollups; they are easy to install and can be opened during periods of only bright light. Or use nice curtains that break the sunlight yet let in some light. Special window trellage, which adds great charm to a building, is superb. Trellises, inexpensive and easy to install, will provide almost per-fect light for plants because they allow alternating shade and light.

Heating

Greenhouse heating used to be a maze of pipes and problems, and only hot water heat was considered acceptable. But many other types of heating are suitable. Installation and operation of the heating unit are not too difficult, but determining what kind of heating fuel to use—gas, oil, or electricity—can be tricky.

Before you select the heating system for your greenhouse, check local gas and electric rates. Decide which will be the most economical, and then investigate specific systems. For my small greenhouse I used forced hot-air heat by extending one duct from the house furnace. A professional installed the duct for $60. Three ducts (for the average greenhouse) from your house furnace would cost no more than $400.

The warm-air–gas-fired heater, which has a safety pilot and thermostatic controls, is good. Provide masonry or metal chimneys so fumes are released outside. A nonvented heater does not

A hygrometer and a thermometer are used in this greenhouse to measure temperature and humidity. (Photo by Matthew Barr)

need an outlet chimney; the combustible chamber is sealed and outside the greenhouse. The heater extends about 10 inches inside the greenhouse and needs only a 17- x 20-inch wall opening. Both types of heaters are available at greenhouse dealers.

The warm-air–oil-fired heater is small, able to fit under a greenhouse bench. It provides sufficient heat for average-sized greenhouses. It has a gun-type burner, a blower, a two-stage fuel pump, and full controls. This heater requires a masonry chimney or a metal smokestack above the roof.

Electric heaters are also satisfactory for small greenhouses. These automatic units have a circulating fan, but heavy-duty electrical lines are necessary. The heater and thermostats should be installed by a professional in accordance with local electric codes.

WHAT YOU CAN GROW

In your greenhouse you can grow almost any plant by the soil-less garden method. Vegetables are of prime consideration; some of the easy ones like lettuce, tomatoes, and cucumbers are sure to be a success, even for the novice. House plants will flourish, and of course you can grow annuals and perennials for outdoor growing to get a headstart on spring. There is little limitation to the kind of plants you can have in the controlled environment of the greenhouse.

You will find plants grow faster and are more healthy than many soil-grown plants, and insect problems, which can become paramount in regular gardening, are of minimum concern in the aqua garden method.

The scope of experimentation is widened; you can experiment with plants that would not adapt indoors, such as tropical house plants, and the more difficult flowers you might want to grow.

Even a homemade greenhouse like this can be used to grow plants in soil-less garden method. (Photo by Matthew Barr)

Zucchini, marigolds, and eggplant grow in this hydroponic garden. Aggregate in plastic boxes can be seen at the front and aluminum foil was used against greenhouse wall to reflect light. (Photo courtesy Sacramento Bee) By permission of Lowell Aitken.

The plastic greenhouse dome works well in moderate climates to grow vegetables as well as annuals and perennials. It is all done in soil-less culture using nutrient solutions. A ventilating fan and electric heater are shown here as part of the greenhouse equipment. (Photo courtesy Sacramento Bee) By permission of Lowell Aitken.

Spinach, cucumbers, and squash grow lushly in nutrient solutions in aggregate in this greenhouse. Note the plastic tubes at ends of white boxes as drain outlets. Containers are elevated off floor to avoid insect problems. (Photo courtesy Sacramento Bee) *By permission of Lowell Aitken.*

Books to Read

Chemical Gardening for the Amateur, Charles N. Connors and Victor A. Tiedjens, Wm. H. Wise Co., 1931

Gardening Without Soil, C. A. Pearson Ltd. London, 1939

Growing Plants Without Soil, D. R. Matlin, Chemical Publishing Corp., N.Y., 1939

Hydroponics, Sholto Douglas, Oxford University Press, London, 1951. Reprinted 1972

The Complete Guide to Soilless Gardening, W. F. Gericke, Prentice Hall Inc., N.Y., 1940

Soilless Culture, Country Life Publications Ltd., London, 1953

Some of the above books are out of print but may be obtained from local libraries.

Bulletins

Gericke, W. F. "Aquaculture," *American Journal of Botany*, Vol. 16, 1929, p. 862

Hanan, J. J., and Holley, W. D., "Introduction of Hydroponics in Colorado," *Agriculture Meteor*, Vol. 7, 1970, pp. 29–38

Hanan, J. J., and Holley, W. D., "Hydroponics," Dept. of Horticulture, Colorado State University, Fort Collins, 1974

Hoagland, Dr., and Arnon, D. F., "Water Culture Method for Growing Plants Without Soil," California Agricultural Experiment Circular 347, University of California, Davis, Ca., 1950

Withrow, R. B., and Withrow, A. P., "Nutriculture," Indiana Agricultural Experimentation Station, Sd-328, Purdue University, Lafayette, Indiana

Suppliers

American Clay Workers, 857 Bryant, Denver, Colorado 80204

Gloeckner, Inc., 15 East 26th Street, New York, N.Y. 10010

Van Waters and Rogers, Inc., 4300 Holly, Denver, Colorado 80200

Pan American Hydroponics, Inc., P.O. Box 470, Grapevine, Texas 76051

Hydroculture Inc., 1516 North 7th Ave., Phoenix, Arizona 85007

Frank Group, 330 Washington St., Marina del Rey, California 90291

Hydro-Garden Chem-Gro, P.O. Box 7172, Colorado Springs, Colorado 80933

Miracle Gardens, Inc., 120 Broadway, New York, N.Y. 10001

Note: Listing of names here is no guarantee of availability of supply as some companies are wholesale; however, they can usually direct you to a source of supply. Also, check your local yellow pages of the phone book under headings such as Chemical Suppliers and general Plant Nurseries. At this writing several new companies are starting operation in hydrocultural supplies and ads for these new companies will no doubt appear in garden magazines in the near future.

Institutions and Organizations Engaged in Hydroculture Research

Alabama Polytechnic Institute

Department of Agriculture, Beltsville, Maryland

Kansas Agricultural Experimentation Station

New Jersey Experimentation Station

Ohio Agricultural Experimentation Station

University of California, Dept. of Soils and Plant Nutrition

University of Florida Agricultural Experimentation Service

University of Illinois, Dept. of Agronomy, Urbana, Illinois

Colorado State University, Dept. of Horticulture, Fort Collins, Colorado